MW01255837

Elevate

Mentoring Toolkit

Taking your life to the next level

Elevate

————

Mentoring Toolkit

A faith-based, mentoring program designed to help
survivors of sex trafficking overcome
past experiences and excel into their futures.

Rebecca Bender
and
Kathy Bryan

Copyright © 2017 Rebecca Bender and Kathy Bryan
All rights reserved.

ISBN: 1544173180
ISBN 13: 9781544173184

Dedication

To my fellow survivor sisters and friends: may you find grace, resilience and abundance in the new things God has in store for you. I pray this toolkit gives you a bit of all of those along the way toward what God has in store for you. You were born for greatness!

~Rebecca Bender

My Lord: The most precious, amazing gift I've received in my life, is the love and salvation you have bestowed on me. I thank you for the amazing journey that is my life, and the trust you placed in me when you called me to serve you.

Keith: Nearly 32 years later, you are still my best friend, most amazing man, and husband a woman could pray for. Thank you for walking through this life with me. I treasure your love, marvel at your intelligence, and revel in your affection.

Lauren, Andrea, Mathew: They say the biggest blessings are often the unexpected ones. Three times in my life my heart exploded with a love I'd never known, or thought existed. Your presence in my life is such a delightful gift. I am forever blessedly honored God chose me to be your mother.

My amazing fellow survivors: Please know this, there is NO shame in what you have experienced. The shame belongs to them; lay it down. Hold your head high, for you my friend, are a magnificent warrior. I pray you quickly embrace the healing the Lord has for you. This earthly journey you are on is burgeoning with freedom, wonder, and a purpose you could never imagine. It's time to unwrap His gifts.

~Kathy Bryan

Special Thanks:

We are so very thankful for the continued support of all our allies, advocates and friends. This book would not have been made possible if it were not for the editing eye of Megan Brown and Chareissa Newbold

Books recommended for this course are:

Bender, Rebecca. (2013). *Roadmap to Redemption*. Createspace.
Maxwell, John. (2018). *Developing the Leader Within You*. Nashville, TN: Thomas Nelson
Unless specified, all Bible verses cited are from the *New International Version*

Contents

Introduction

WELCOME TO ELEVATE!

This Mentoring Toolkit is designed to help you take your life to the next level. It's a 16-module lesson plan that you are able to use in many ways, including:

- Group class in a residential facility or drop in center
- One-on-one with a counselor, mentor or friend
- In our online program: Elevate Academy
- On your own

We do recommend two additional books as a point of reference throughout this 16-module lesson plan. **Phase One will review Roadmap to Redemption.**

Basic Overview

Phase One guides survivors over an eight module period as they work through Roadmap to Redemption. The material and questions in the book and this curriculum are designed to take the student into deeper levels of healing.

Phase Two journeys through basic business etiquette and professionalism, helping better prepare students for their future dreams and how to actually obtain them.

Phase Three delves into the importance of leadership. Students will learn what leadership truly is, how to be a great leader, and begin to explore the talents hidden within them. This can be geared toward being a leader in the home, community or the workplace.

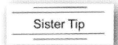 Boxes will help indicate an important tip or insight.

Throughout the 16 modules, you will also be encouraged to participate in the **Activities** section, the **Homework** assignments and you are welcome to join our online **Elevate Connect** community of survivors from all over the world. The more you put into this program, the more you'll get out of it. By the end of these 16 modules, you'll have a clearer understanding of the goals you want to accomplish, steps to get there and areas within yourself that need to be strengthened to maintain it.

Teacher & Mentor Guide

Dear Mentor,

Thank you for choosing to be here, in this moment, dedicating your time and talents to walking alongside survivors. Mentoring, while not always easy, is quite rewarding. This 16-module program is designed to take the student through three phases of study, with your guidance and encouragement.

Over the last several years, we have mentored hundreds of survivors of human trafficking, gleaning a lot of experience and wisdom over that time period that we would like to share with you before beginning this journey.

Helping people can be enjoyable, rewarding work. There are times when it can also be difficult and messy, and even painful. Just as no two people are the same, and no two experiences identical, no two healing journeys will evolve in the same way either. Some come to the program ready to dive in, no matter the cost, stripping away all that has held them back from truly exploring their life. Others, though they have the same desire, do not have quite the drive or abandon to throw themselves in so wholeheartedly.

This occurs for a wide variety of reasons; none wrong, just different. We must choose to encourage and point out the potential we see, allowing them to drive their own destinies. When we cross the line, trying to make healing happen, we do no good at all. In fact, we harm. Humbly, I submit to you that when anyone tries to control another, even for apparent good reason, they have slipped into the same tactics the survivor experienced with the trafficker. **Freedom and control cannot co-exist.**

Things to Remember

- No two survivors are the same.
- Survivors have different personalities, just like everyone else.
  - Different personalities react to trauma and adversity differently.

- "Compliant, quiet, withdrawn Nancy" is no more traumatized than "Bad Attitude Betty" with her angry responses, outspoken, boisterous behavior. Both are deserving of our help.
- Extroverts and introverts each need time to share within the cohort, being aware that usually an introvert is unlikely to interrupt or interject amidst a lively conversation. Make sure each person has time to share and have their voices heard.
- Lose your expectations...let God lead.
- Let God fulfill you...not the work!
- Empower ... not fix, you are not the Holy Spirit. Let Him do what He does best.
  - The only one doing any fixing is God and the client. We "get" to empower, encourage and exhort...that is all, and it's a privilege.
  - Survivors have a voice; it was silenced. Encourage them to speak up.
  - Honor their voice, opinions, and values (even if they aren't yours).
  - Love conquers all.

Beauty of the Cohort

Embarking upon this journey with a cohort is an added benefit. This small group of people will be addressing some of the biggest traumas of their lives simultaneously. Having a person or persons that 'get it' is unparalleled. This is not to say that people who haven't survived trafficking can't be supportive. It does remove the added pressure of feeling like every feeling, revelation, or question has to be explained.

Even so, statements like these are repeatedly heard from clients. "Nobody will understand." "I'm weird," or "I'm bad." These wrong beliefs keep survivors locked in isolation, imprisoned by guilt or shame, hindering growth. So, without breaking confidentiality, it is our role to encourage them to take the step of entrusting the group with their "weird", thing, helping them realize that several persons within this group have the exact same sentiments. Many, if not all, in the group often assume that what they are feeling, experiencing or dealing with, is too much for someone else to understand.

The cohort also provides a safe place. Time after time we have heard that *this* small group is the first place the survivor has felt and seen authentic, unconditional love lived out. This is huge! Even if their family wasn't the trafficker, statistically speaking, most survivors come from difficult homes, many where love had strings attached. Having a safe place to experience healthy relational love between friends is a gift.

Healing

We tend to hear the word "restore" in this line of work. However, it's important to remember that many survivors have been abused prior to their trafficking experience, many even in infancy and toddler years. This means they quite literally don't have anything to restore. For these individuals, healing means "building" a foundation of "normal" where none existed before. They must learn the dynamics of healthy relationships in which being controlled never belongs.

Trust

Be honest, no matter what. I know this sounds like, "Well, duh!" Honesty, however, is so incredibly important because these clients have been continually betrayed and manipulated in the most devastating ways. Life has taught them the lies that no one is trustworthy; they can only trust themselves. Many survivors exist with the belief that everyone, even when they are being nice and seemingly have no ill motive, really wants something from them. *We just don't know what that something is yet.*

So, how does this play into mentoring? Well, be sure that what you say, is what you do. Do not tell a client something they want to hear if you aren't sure you can follow through on what you said.

For example, don't say you will be somewhere or do something if you don't have 100% intention of doing it. For instance, don't leave a session with a "See you next module!" if you aren't definitely sure you will be the one mentoring the next module. Instead, say something like, "Great seeing you today! Can't wait until next time." Being thoughtful around your word choice is imperative when mentoring survivors.

Mentors will mess up, give yourself grace. But we can also strive to be a person whose behavior aids the mentee in learning to trust again. Say you forget to send some material you promised to find. When you realize it, apologize, and then go ahead and follow through. Learning that healthy people own their mistakes and fix them, are still able to be trusted, and are as imperfect as everyone else, is also a valuable lesson.

Boundaries

Healthy boundaries are a crucial element to relational health, and they are often non-existent to our clients. When everything has been taken from you, and you feel like an object having been stripped of all basic human rights, boundaries no longer apply. They aren't respected or even noticed. You have no rights to even set them. Anyone emerging from this type of situation will understandably need to learn what healthy boundaries are, and it will take time to establish them.

One way our clients begin building healthy boundaries is by seeing healthy boundaries walked out. Our interactions and the way we treat others should model healthy boundaries.

These boundaries pertain not only to healthy communication, but also in regards to sharing personal experiences. As students navigate life after trafficking, assessing what and how much to share and in what ways is imperative. Not only is it an important lesson in learning to honor yourself, it is an integral part of learning how to avoid exploitation.

Boundaries are not a bunch of arbitrary rules to keep someone from having fun. I have found it helpful to explain that boundaries are not there to tell you what *not* to do. They are meant to provide safety. Just like a fence along a cliff, they are meant to allow freedom, but prevent disaster. One way that I typically share the boundary is by first starting out with the "why" we have the set rule. *Why's* must preface everything we say.

Self-Care

Self-care is essential. It is healthy. It is deserved. It keeps us functioning on all cylinders. If we don't maintain proper self-care, not only are we not modeling it well for our clients, we are risking burnout. Having already been injured enough by their experiences, we do not want to add to their burdens or pain by trying to work with them in the midst of our burnout or in an unhealthy manner, nor do we want to lose the joy we find in mentoring.

Confidentiality

It is critical to maintain strict confidentiality. Every survivor is going to be different, especially when they are first out of the life, rarely knowing if they want or need confidentiality or anonymity. At this point, they are still beginning to process that they were, in fact, trafficked rather than experiencing the effects of a series of bad choices.

Having just begun the healing process, they often are not prepared to make a decision regarding their own confidentiality or how much, if any, of their story they want to share. So, we need to help with that. I DO NOT mean forcing them to share or not share their experiences. I mean modeling proper confidentiality for them. Whatever they tell us goes nowhere. This respect for confidentiality aids them in learning how to protect themselves and to be considerate of their own interests.

With that being said, one thing we need to consider and plan for, as mentors and teachers, is how to deal with what we've heard and still maintain confidentiality. Many people are verbal processors. Even if they are not, we are going to hear things we wish we hadn't when working with people who have been so heinously abused. I fully realize every day is not going to be full of horrific stories; we have a curriculum to teach. However, it will happen. We do NOT want to get "numb" to atrocities.

It's ok if your heart breaks. It should! It breaks God's heart too. So, we feel it is essential to have a plan or procedure in place for mentor "debriefing" or "venting." I suggest journaling, without including identifiers, or having a person within your team to talk with, again, without identifiers. This is not only proper self-care but also models confidentiality and boundaries.

Expect – Redirect – Edify

In regards to unacceptable behaviors, survivors are people like everyone else. Expect from them the things you expect from others. We humans often fail to realize that we will receive the behavior we expect. If we expect them to participate, be real, be punctual, and be courteous, more often than not, that's what we will get. When at all possible, reframe or redirect negative thinking. Negative thinking is an enormous habit to overcome, but it can be done. If you find yourself having negative emotions it may be time to take a sabbatical, pursue self-care time or try another department within your org until you feel refreshed. Always be honoring, even when they are not. As mentors, we have the opportunity to make a great impression on the lives of our clients while lovingly enforcing expectations.

Be genuine, and generous with your praise. Hearing good things has most likely been rare. Too much edification is virtually impossible. You will NOT make them egomaniacs. Conversely, when there is something that needs to be addressed, be kind, direct, and succinct with your feedback, as well as pointing out any positives you can. Anyone who has been through any sort of professional training may have heard of the compliment critique sandwich. This is especially needed when learning to be a mentor. If you need to address an issue, ensure you wedge it in between compliments, genuine compliments. Research has shown when the feedback received by a person is overwhelmingly negative, compliments are rarely seen as genuine. Again, this is part of a thought process. It makes perfect sense, when a person isn't used to hearing something positive, for them to doubt compliments, or distrust them. Thankfully, the more we all hear them, the more we see truth walked out, the more a new path is created that slowly allows in the good.

Time

I believe respecting other's time is most often the most difficult boundary to maintain with clients. Because often times, the people we are working with are not used to having someone who truly cares, there occasionally are some that tend to want to call you for everything. The tendency for us can be to think, "Geez, this girl is so needy!" But, she's not. She simply isn't used to having someone who actually gives a rip about her. Just like when we meet a new friend that we really click with and want to hang with 24/7, our clients can want to spend more time with us than we have to give.

Establishing parameters at the start will create proper expectations, allowing the client to feel safe and yet protect your personal time, promoting self-care. It will also foster a healthy atmosphere, setting the stage for other relationships to develop in their life.

PHASE ONE

Roadmap to Redemption

MODULE ONE

Introduction & Misidentification

Read: Roadmap to Redemption, Introduction and Chapter One

GROUP SETTING: INTRODUCE yourself, share your location, profession, how long you've been out of the game/the life, or what type of trafficking you've experienced. Share something about yourself such as, "I skydived once" or "I tried taking a painting class to relieve stress."

Before beginning take time to do the following:

- Familiarize everyone with the syllabus for this semester.
- Review the calendar dates and meeting times for your group. Are there any holidays that will require adjusting your scheduled meeting?
- Discuss Mentor's plan as facilitator, and any future guest trainer's role, as needed:
  - Structure, time, meeting place, prayer, expectations, homework
- Milestone Activities
  - Create Dream Board
    - Due by end of module Eight
  - Take "Get to know YOU" online quiz
  - Complete time management sheet
  - Create Mission Statement for life/goals
  - Graduation
    - Certificate of Completion
    - Roadmap for goals that includes mission statement
- How to get the most from Elevate
  1. Complete all assignments prior to the group discussion. Give yourself the time needed to ruminate on the material and respond to the questions.
  2. Attend and participate in all of the group sessions.
  3. Decide within yourself to make the most of this experience, putting into practice what you are learning and facing change head-on with glorious expectation!

- After Graduation Accountability
  - Whether completing this solo or within a group, plan to follow up at three, six, and twelve months after completion to assess the progress you've made in reaching the goals you've set for yourself.

Take time to ensure that everyone has time to go around the room and share introductions as needed.

———

From Kathy:

It was nearly 27 years after my exploitation ended before I learned of human trafficking. I can remember clearly sitting there in my seat perfectly still, as the world around me began to swirl. I felt like I was floating. My mind was replaying the words I had just heard, while bits of memories of my own experience simultaneously circled through my head like a tornado. It was like a cosmic jigsaw puzzle and my thoughts were struggling to fit the pieces together. I didn't want them to fit, but they did. And even more troubling the more I heard, the more seamlessly the pieces all came together. It was bizarre experience, to say the least. One, you may well relate to.

If I had had a more accurate idea of what human trafficking was, I probably would have made that connection much, much sooner. I had never known what to label my experience. I just knew I hated it. No one had kidnapped me, held me captive, or hand cuffed me to a bed in a basement for months on end. I lived at home and still attended school throughout those two long years. No, what happened to me didn't fit any of the stereotypes society is used to, even though it was heinous, and I had felt no more valuable than a piece of used furniture.

If we, the ones affected by this crime don't identify it as human trafficking, who will? Every person involved in human trafficking, the trafficker, the buyer, the victim, is raised in this same culture with the same stereotypes. Educating everyone is imperative, and clearly we need to have mandatory human trafficking education in all schools. If children understand what it is, they will be more likely to identify it, and to seek help if they ever need it.

Roadmap to Redemption Chapter 1 Questions

1. How do **you** think our culture has fueled the misidentification of human trafficking? Why don't victims know they are caught in human trafficking?

_____
_____
_____
_____
_____
_____
_____
_____
_____
_____

Sister Tip

*We encourage those who didn't experience pimp-controlled trafficking **not** to overlook information in the book or to dismiss it as if it doesn't apply. Dig deeper by looking for similarities and differences while reading through. Replace the word pimp with the name of the person who controlled you. Remember, at the core, trafficking is trafficking, coercion, force and fraud took place in every survivor's life.*

2. When planting a seed regarding forgiveness (and I'm not saying this seed needs to grow and flourish NOW), how can we look at SOME buyers and traffickers with the same understanding of being deceived by the enemy into thinking this behavior is socially acceptable and actually glamorized? Do you think there are other ways that culture has deceived young men into growing up thinking buying or selling is ok?

_____
_____
_____
_____
_____
_____
_____
_____
_____
_____

From Rebecca-

In November of 2013 I visited the Washington, DC Holocaust Museum. On the wall hung this profound statement that really resonated with me in this fight to eradicate modern day slavery:

"In 1932 the President of Germany heard about Hitler and the Nazi party that was rising up. After receiving advice from his council, he offered to take Hitler under him, believing that he'd be easier to monitor and control if they had him close. Within one year, Hitler was appointed to Chancellor." So much for that idea, huh president?

So here is something for you to chew on...

If the President of Germany, a smart, older adult, intelligent man, can be manipulated and coerced into giving control to a man that ruined a nation of people, how is it "we" can't understand how one man can use coercion to manipulate and control one vulnerable young woman? You can understand and believe the history of the Nazi party, yet refuse to believe that this type of coercion, fraud and force could convince a girl without handcuffs to sell herself? A girl that is already vulnerable, promiscuous, possibly abused, etc.?

3. Explain your thoughts while reading He Was My Hitler.

_____
_____
_____
_____
_____
_____
_____
_____
_____
_____
_____

4. Did this help you see adults can also be manipulated?

_____
_____
_____
_____
_____

_____

_____

_____

_____

_____

_____

5. In what ways does this passage change how you view your "choice" or responsibility in what happened to you?

_____

_____

_____

_____

_____

_____

_____

_____

_____

_____

_____

6. What aspect of this chapter resonated with you the most?

_____

_____

_____

_____

_____

_____

_____

_____

_____

———

If you were a child, you may not have struggled with the issue of "choice."
Rather you may have struggled with feeling like it was your fault,
that you caused it, or you deserved it. <u>None</u> of these are true!

———

Human Trafficking as defined in the Federal Trafficking Victims Protection Act (TVPA):

"**Trafficking** in persons" and "**human trafficking**" have been used as umbrella terms for the act of recruiting, harboring, transporting, providing, or obtaining a person for compelled labor or commercial sex acts through the use of force, fraud, or coercion.

Below is a Visual Model Depicting the Actions, Means, and Purpose definition of Human Trafficking. Having only one from each circle would constitute a trafficking. The only exception is if the person is a minor being commercially sexually exploited, force, fraud or coercion do not need to be present.

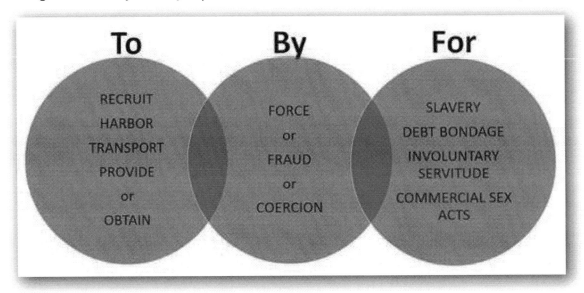

MODULE TWO

Power of Coercion & Red Flags

Read: Roadmap to Redemption, Chapters Two and Three

WARNING! THESE CHAPTERS can be tough, but you can totally do this! Just be sure to allow yourself the grace to take time to process and respond to the information. These questions can be done throughout the week; they do not need to be completed at one time.

Also, it helps to jot down things you'd like to discuss or share with others so that you can bring it up during your in-person discussion session, or within the online community.

Remember: While there is a definite pattern/process, all experiences are individual.

Many of us didn't recognize there was any trouble because our exploitation occurred within a loving "relationship." I thought I was dating the man who ultimately controlled two years of my life. I loved him and I thought he loved me. That was what he wanted me to think. He spent a lot of time crafting that perception. He did everything a girl wants. He listened to me, spent time with me, took me on dates, and for long drives. He gave me the attention I desperately wanted, and wasn't getting at home. Well, in the beginning that is.

Perhaps that isn't what happened for you. Perhaps the person who trafficked you didn't behave that way, and instead used force to traffic you. Maybe it was a family member, or within a gang environment. However it began, there are core truths that tend to apply to all traffickers.

Traffickers are master manipulators. They can and will exploit any vulnerability, using several different tactics to get exactly what they want. They are usually very egocentric, and controlling, and oftentimes disguise that control as 'love.'

Authentic love does not control or cause fear.
Theirs is no fear in love. Perfect love drives out fear. **1 John 4:18**

ACTIVITY: Take this test: http://lovegoodbadugly.com/quiz-is-it-love-or-control/

Roadmap to Redemption Chapter 2 Questions

Working through the memories of first being turned out can be hard. Questions like these ran through my mind. Why wasn't I enough? What more could I do to make him love me? I wanted friends and felt alone. Bitterness, anger and rage took root in my heart.

1. Looking back at your experience, what patterns of manipulation and control did you identify? How did it loosely follow the "dating, grooming, turning out, breaking" pattern discussed in the chapter?

_____

_____

_____

_____

_____

_____

_____

_____

_____

_____

2. If your experience was familial, what parts of the pattern described in the book can you "see" within your specific situation? Note: The bond normally created during the "grooming" phase is already in place in a family setting.

_____

_____

_____

_____

_____

_____

_____

_____

_____

3. Though painful, how was examining this process helpful?

_____

_____

_____

_____

_____

_____

_____

_____

_____

Roadmap to Redemption Chapter 3 Questions

The coercion traffickers use can be so subtle that we completely overlook it, even now when we are out of the exploitation. The life of my baby sister was threatened the entire time I was trafficked. In fact, this was the number one reason I was compliant. I totally believed him. My family was kept under surveillance. He always knew what was happening with them. He also used false promises, and force to control me, and sleep deprivation was a way of life. There were, of course, many other tactics he used and other factors from my upbringing that made me as vulnerable as I was.

What I would like you to see is that during the exploitation, it is very difficult to recognize what is happening. If it were obvious, we'd run right away before we got too deeply involved with them. Think of it this way, their livelihood depended upon deceiving us so convincingly they'd be able to have ultimate control. Being deceived is not a crime, nor something to be ashamed of. ALL the shame belongs squarely on their shoulders, not ours!

Before you move to the next question, please take a few minutes to consider and complete the following activity.

ACTIVITY: Think of a child you know and care about. It could be a niece, nephew, family friend, or your own child. Now, think of your personal experience happening to them. Would you think it was something they caused, was their fault, or blame them? Jot down how this makes you feel and any insights it provides.

4. Coercion is a HUGE part of human trafficking and often, one hard to identify or explain. When reading through all of the coercion methods, how many were you able to circle?

In what ways did learning about the power of coercion and circling the tactics that took place in your personal experience help you?

_____

_____

_____

_____

_____
_____
_____
_____
_____
_____
_____

ACTIVITY: One memory you have from your experience is probably harder than others right now. Close your eyes, focus on that memory, and ask, "Jesus, where are you in that memory?"

Give yourself time to focus and hear His response. Note what you saw and the feelings it caused.

It is highly likely this was a tough module. In addition to the questions above, you may find these points or topics come up in today's discussion.

1. Were you able to identify the four stages within your personal experience?
   - Dating and grooming
   - Brainwashing/manipulation; gaining trust and information to use against a person at a later time; filling a need, exploiting vulnerabilities, isolation
   - Turning out and breaking
2. Coercion- the act of persuading someone to do something
3. Can be very subtle or blatantly obvious
4. Do the childhood risk factors discussed on page 36 (paragraph 4) ring true? Are there others not listed?

Breaking Myths & Stages of Recovery

Read: Roadmap to Redemption, Chapters Four and Five

Roadmap to Redemption Chapter 4 Questions

CHANGING THE MINDSET of our culture begins with ourselves. The truth is we grew up in the same culture that views trafficking as something that happens "over there." Which is one reason why we were so easily deceived. Breaking those perceptions and allowing truth into our minds is imperative. We all have many broken mindsets that need the renewing that can only come from God and knowing truth.

One of these myths or mindsets, is the belief the situation we found ourselves in was our choice. It is certainly better for them if we believe we brought all of this on ourselves. And that belief creates doubt within us, self-loathing, anger, depression, and makes it difficult to trust our decision-making skills. Hopefully, with all you are learning, the realization they chose you is becoming evident, challenging and changing this myth in your heart and mind.

After being 'chosen' or targeted by your pimp, your family member or whoever trafficked you, is it surprising to know that you were Chosen by God? He chose to create you; wonderfully, beautifully, uniquely. You are a treasure to Him, and He longs for you to give Him first place in your life. I fully realize that putting someone else first in your life may be a thoroughly scary proposition. But, consider this, when He chose you it was for divine purpose, to bless you abundantly, to be a friend, and have you be His friend. It was not for evil, or self-serving purposes, like when our exploiters chose us. And, best of all, even though He has chosen us, we *get* to decide to choose Him!

1. Having made it through Chapter 4, do you have a 'before and after' image or understanding of trafficking? Explain.

   _____

   _____

   _____

   _____

The Lord has given us an amazingly detailed and poignant love letter in providing us the scriptures. They are not simply a book of rules. They are living truths full of wisdom.

Psalms 40 speaks not only of the amazing things God does for us in our times of need, but shows how we can call to Him from any place and He will hear. It speaks of His incredible faithfulness, provision, and love.

Psalms 40:1-17

1. *I waited patiently for the Lord to help me, and he turned to me and heard my cry.*
2. *He lifted me out of the pit of despair, out of the mud and the mire. He set my feet on solid ground and steadied me as I walked along.*
3. *He has given me a new song to sing, a hymn of praise to our God. Many will see what he has done and be amazed. They will put their trust in the Lord.*
4. *Oh, the joys of those who trust the Lord, who have no confidence in the proud or in those who worship idols.*
5. *O Lord my God, you have performed many wonders for us. Your plans for us are too numerous to list. You have no equal. If I tried to recite all your wonderful deeds, I would never come to the end of them.*
6. *You take no delight in sacrifices or offerings. Now that you have made me listen, I finally understand - you don't require burnt offerings or sin offerings.*
7. *Then I said, "Look, I have come. As is written about me in the Scriptures:*
8. *I take joy in doing your will, my God, for your instructions are written on my heart."*
9. *I have told all your people about your justice. I have not been afraid to speak out, as you, O Lord, well know.*
10. *I have not kept the good news of your justice hidden in my heart; I have talked about your faithfulness and saving power. I have told everyone in the great assembly of your unfailing love and faithfulness.*
11. *Lord, don't hold back your tender mercies from me. Let your unfailing love and faithfulness always protect me.*

12. *For troubles surround me—too many to count! My sins pile up so high I can't see my way out. They outnumber the hairs on my head. I have lost all courage.*
13. *Please, Lord, rescue me! Come quickly, Lord, and help me.*
14. *May those who try to destroy me humiliated and put to shame. May those who take delight in my trouble turn back in disgrace.*
15. *Let them be horrified by their shame, for they said, "Aha! We've got him now!"*
16. *But may all who search for you be filled with joy and gladness in you. May those who love your salvation repeatedly shout, "The Lord is great!"*
17. *As for me, since I am poor and needy, let the Lord keep me in his thoughts. You are my helper and my savior. O my God, do not delay.*

2. What was your favorite verse from Psalms Chapter 40? Was it hard to pick a favorite? What do you think God is saying to you through that verse?

_____
_____
_____
_____
_____
_____
_____
_____
_____
_____
_____

Another myth I want to break is that you will be excited and happy to be "rescued" and ready for the healing process. The opposite is usually true. In fact, I recently watched the new Star Wars movie, and found it interesting the robots were programmed to say, "Congratulations! You are being rescued. Please do not resist." I'm sure to most people in that theater, that seemed like a completely inane statement. The truth is that often times, we don't realize how very much we need help or rescuing.

We all seem to know when our friends need it, though, don't we? And best of all, God knew just how much we needed rescuing. That is why He sent Jesus. We were created to serve Him; to live in communion with Him. That void in our lives, the hole we try to fill with so many different things, only one thing fits there. It is a God-sized hole. Until we fill it with the very thing that fits, we will have the empty, "something is missing" feeling inside. It is so very indescribable when that feeling is gone, totally sated.

Over the course of our lives, we have tried many things to fill that hole. In the process, our personal boundaries have been expanded to unhealthy limits. It will take a little time, but those boundary lines can be rebuilt providing you with safe, healthy limits that bring freedom and self-preservation. That's what healthy boundaries do. They are meant to keep us safe, not restrict us. Healthy boundaries are protective, not punitive.

3. Below is the boundary box discussed in chapter four. List how you would label the boxes.

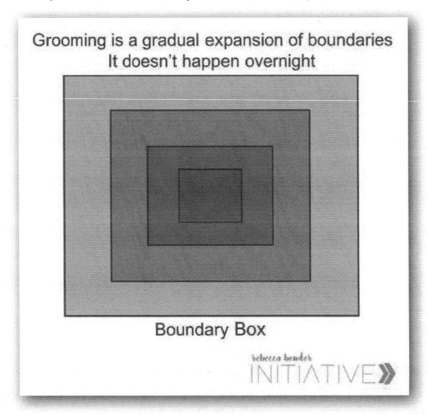

Grooming is a gradual expansion of boundaries
It doesn't happen overnight

Boundary Box

rebecca bender
INITIATIVE »

Now that you have identified some things that stretched your boundaries let's look for behaviors or "boundary pangs" that need to healed. Recognizing and healing them is an integral part of the process.

4. How did you identify with each pang discussed in chapter four? List any others not listed.

- Hardened
- Drag
- Denial
- Hope
- Structure

Think of that ONE boundary pang that you struggle with the most. Think back in your mind to another time you felt exactly that same way. Describe that memory. Continue going back in your mind until you get as far back as you remember, uncovering each time you felt the same way. Document each time here:

_____
_____
_____
_____
_____
_____
_____
_____
_____
_____
_____

The very last memory of that "boundary pang" or feeling, is where it took root in your heart. We want to pray the blood of Jesus over that issue that took root. We want to fill that place up with the Lord's Holy Spirit, and mostly, we want to release the person who harmed us from any responsibility of planting that within us. Unforgiveness only gives birth to sin. We want complete freedom!

WE WERE CHOSEN... BY GOD!
We do have success and purpose birthed in our hearts and spirits, but it is a God-given desire that has been tainted by the things of this world.

Roadmap to Redemption Chapter 5 Questions
Whew! You have made it through chapter four. What a journey you have been on so far. We are so proud of you. We have faith you can continue on this path with great success ahead of you! It may be hard, but it is worth it!! Just like building a new road, you are making new neuropathways in your brain, or new patterns of behavior. The more you use those new behaviors, the more it becomes permanent, slowly replacing the old one. Soon, these 'new' ways will be second nature to you. So, keep going! You can do this!

You have now arrived at one of our very favorite parts of the program. Discovering your dreams and preparing to create your Dream Board. We all have a God-given purpose planted in our hearts. It's time to unearth yours. As you move to the next steps below, stop for a moment and ask the Holy Spirit for revelation.

By mainly focusing on all the dreams and goals that God has given you, you are now prepared to work on your dream board due at end of Phase 1.

The purpose of the Dream Boards is to discover the dreams planted within us by God. Including them on our dream board is a way of acknowledging them. We will use our boards to provide focus and clarity in setting goals and encouraging ourselves to attain them. Including inspirational things is ok, but the point is to locate and document dreams.

Let's look at pages 73-74.

1. If both resources and time were unlimited, what would you do with your life?

_____
_____
_____
_____
_____
_____
_____
_____
_____
_____
_____

Read *Psalm 50:10* – "All the beasts of the forest are mine; and the
cattle on one thousand hills."

2. List three dreams God wants to accomplish THROUGH you.

_____
_____
_____
_____
_____
_____
_____
_____
_____
_____

3. What are the personal habits you need to create/change to fulfill those goals?

_____
_____
_____

_____
_____
_____
_____
_____
_____
_____
_____

4. Using the **Goal Chart**, create steps you will take to accomplish these goals.

My Goals this year!		Date:	
Goal	48 hour plan	Short term plan	Long term plan
Lose 20 pounds	Stock kitchen with only foods I can eat. Decide on exercise program	Workout every other day 1500 cal/day	Maintain weight loss by continuing to exercise at least 3x's module. Eat 1800 cal/day
Get bachelor's degree	Meet with admission counselor apply for financial aid and scholarships	Schedule set study times Join a study group Maintain B+ avg or higher	

Midterm: Create your personal dream board and submit it by the end of Module 7.

Use your creativity, and use a method that speaks to you. Some use a poster board or bulletin board, while others use PowerPoint to make one. The sky's the limit.

While things that inspire you are ok to include, remember this is to help you define, and ultimately, reach the purposes God has for your life.

Once complete, this is something you want to place where you will see it often, preferably daily. Also, be sure to share these plans you are making with those important people in your life. They will not only be excited, but they will help pointing you in the direction of your dreams until they become reality.

Dream Board Brainstorming Ideas

People of Value and Purpose:

Psalms 139:16 "All the days ordained for me were written in your book before one of them came to be."
Jeremiah 29:11 "For I know the plans I have for you, says the Lord, thoughts and plans for welfare and peace, and not for evil, to give you hope in your final outcome."

Moving forward with your dreams

1. Give yourself permission to dream.
2. Discover your dreams.
3. Write them down! If a dream board isn't your thing, then journal about it, create a sign, write a song, create a commercial, anything!
4. Find a scripture to claim as your own. Check out Isaiah 55:11, Psalms 37:4, Psalms 103:5, Psalms 145:19, Proverbs 10:24, Proverbs 11:23, Proverbs 13:4,
5. Remind yourself that just because satan looks like he is winning the battle, that doesn't mean he has won the war.
6. Stand in faith.
7. Start small.
8. Don't pull back because it's easier to stay where you are.
9. Break some oppressive rules.
10. Change your attitude.

Undoing the Brainwash

Read: Roadmap to Redemption, Chapter Six

BRAINWASHED? THAT SEEMS extreme, doesn't it? That is exactly what happened to most of us, though. The person controlling us used tactics that literally changed the way we thought, creating patterns of belief that were false, unhealthy, and also lead to bad habits. We need and deserve to have those mindsets and lies washed from our thinking. True freedom means living in truth.

 **Points to Ponder**

- Breaking bad habits takes effort on your part. Make a conscious choice. When we know what to do but, choose not to, that is a sin.
- Taking thoughts captive and subjecting them to Christ.
- Iron sharpens iron

"As iron sharpens iron, so one person sharpens another." - Proverbs 27:17

Roadmap to Redemption Chapter 6 Questions

1. Life is surrounded with people: it's just how it is. Real life interaction will prepare us for the real world. We must learn healthy interaction. How do you think God teaches us to interact with people?

_____
_____
_____
_____
_____
_____
_____
_____
_____

In school, we may have attended a math class, read through the lesson book and listened to the teacher in front instruct us. In your Christian walk, this is not necessarily the case.

Yes, God gives us a lesson book: THE BIBLE. However, He then allows situations to arise in our lives to sharpen us, to teach us, and to allow us to practice. Think of that as God giving you homework.

2. What are some habits/characteristics in yourself that you'd like to change?

_____
_____
_____
_____
_____
_____
_____
_____
_____
_____
_____

ACTIVITY: Think of one habit or characteristic. Can you pinpoint a memory of when you felt that way last? Ask the Holy Spirit to show you the memory before that. Now, the memory before that? Is that the last memory you have of feeling that way? If not keep going back until it is. Let's pull that weed and replace it by asking the Holy Spirit to fill your heart and release the opposite! List the opposite characteristics of your responses above in question 2.

_____
_____
_____
_____
_____
_____
_____
_____
_____
_____

3. What lies do you still believe?

_____
_____
_____

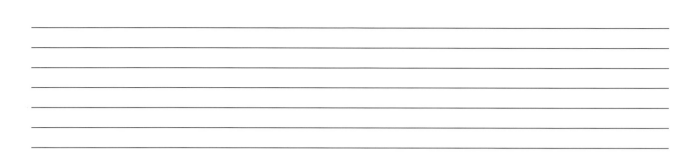

Discuss this and post your response within the group forum.

Changing Your THOUGHT Life

2 Corinthians 10: 3-6 (The Message)
"The world is unprincipled. It's dog-eat-dog out there! The world doesn't fight fair. But we don't live or fight our battles that way—never have and never will. The tools of our trade aren't for marketing or manipulation, but they are for demolishing that entire massively corrupt culture. We use our powerful God-tools for smashing warped philosophies, tearing down barriers erected against the truth of God, fitting every loose thought and emotion and impulse into the structure of life shaped by Christ. Our tools are ready at hand for clearing the ground of every obstruction and building lives of obedience into maturity."

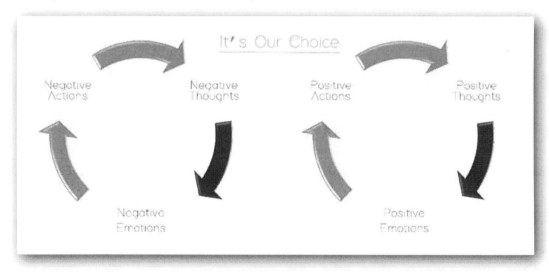

Ever wish you could feel more joyful, free, positive and happy? Are you tired of feeling like you have no control over your thoughts, your emotions and your life?

We used to be controlled by someone else but no longer. Being controlled was something we couldn't control. Because of that experience, we have a habit of feeling out of control of our own lives. We need to break that habit. We are in control. It is OUR life. We can do this. So, how?

First we must recognize a few truths:

THOUGHTS- Our thought life and our emotional life are intricately tied to each other. Negative thoughts lead to negative feelings which lead to negative thoughts which lead to negative feelings thus creating a cycle. Living in this cycle nearly always makes a person feel they are at the mercy of their feelings. However, you CAN control your feelings rather than allowing them to control you. Learning to choose the thoughts you allow in your mind is empowering. Further, replacing those negative thoughts with truthful, positive messages breaks the cycle, reprogramming your thought life. The Scripture teaches us that we are what we think.

God knew what we thought in our heart would dictate who we become.

Proverbs 23:7 - "As a man thinks in his heart, so is he…"

God knew our minds would need renewal and transformation.

Romans 12:2 - "Do not be conformed to this world, but be transformed by the renewing of your mind."

God knew we would need to control what we focus on.

Philippians 4:8 "Finally brothers whatever is true, honorable, just, pure, lovely, commendable, if there is any excellence, anything worthy of praise, think about these things." ESV

ATTITUDES- Our behavior helps determines our attitude. Attitudes are nothing more than habits of thoughts put to action, simply deciding to "Just Do It," as Nike® used to say. We have to act/behave how we want, and then we will begin to feel like doing so, not the other way around.

For example, many people want or wish they could lose weight but never quite "feel" like changing the way they eat. Recently, we chose to radically change the way my husband and I ate because we wanted to see if we could get rid of his diabetes. I personally had never had any luck losing weight, but I chose to do this despite how I felt.

After two weeks of changed eating habits, I had a different attitude. I no longer only chose these eating changes; I liked them and had a positive attitude about them. My behavior and positive thoughts towards my behavior changed my attitude. One last example, parents often find themselves telling their children to get a grateful attitude. Those statements aren't usually very fruitful. However, if you help them change their behavior, say by having them genuinely compliment everyone in the household once a day, an attitude change soon comes along.

Basically, if we…

- Say the right words
- Read the right books
- Listen to the right things

- Hang out with the right people
- Do the right things
- Pray the right prayers

…our attitudes will change! It's making the conscious choice to control ourselves, our behaviors, our feelings, and our attitudes that affects that change.

Know whose voice you are listening to:

God's Voice	Satan's Voice
Calms	Obsesses
Comforts	Worries
Convicts	Condemns
Encourages	Discourages
Enlightens	Confuses
Leads	Pushes
Reassures	Frightens
Stills	Rushes

MODULE FIVE

Spiritual Warfare

Read: Roadmap to Redemption, Chapter Seven

HI, THERE! CAN you believe it's already module five? It goes by quickly, doesn't it? There are loads of gold nuggets in this chapter that are all truly valuable. I'd like to leave you with these additional truths to consider as well.

Remember, Jesus is the absolute center of everything. Any thoughts that we have that do not line up with His truth are lies. Lies have zero power unless we give them power by acknowledging and following them. We need to bring Jesus into the center of every single situation we are in because the enemy is at war against the truths of God. His agenda is to tear down the truths of God and trample them. The only 'power' he has, is the power we give him when we believe the lies he spins. Remember these two things:

- God's opposite is not satan. He is simply a created being, just as we are.   He is the opposite of Michael the archangel, not God.
- The enemy is not omnipresent, nor omniscient, or nor omnipotent.

The way out of the battle is The Word. It's your weapon and your comfort. The Word is Jesus, and even He used the Word, Scripture, to fight the enemy when He was tempted. It is vital that we build our relationship with the Word, and that we spend time in the Word. Knowing truth will build us up, enabling us to stop giving power to the powerless lies spewed at us. We all have lies that were told to us so much they literally became strongholds, walls, within us. The only thing empowering those walls is believing the lie.

So, concentrating the truth like an intense laser beam on the walls of those lies will explode it. Here's one example: Lie- "You are good for nothing. You're just a _____." Fill in the blank with whatever you were told. There are many stupid lies, but truth prevails! Break that wall down with this: Truth: "I am chosen, holy and blameless before God."

Ephesians 1:4: "For He chose us in Christ before the foundation of the world that we may be holy and unblemished in His sight in love."

I know this is new thinking, but you can do this. Lies are the enemy's weapons intended to destroy our souls and drown out the voice of the One who cherishes us and can never stop whispering our names. Since Jesus already defeated him, let's not entertain his schemes. Let's live free!

No warrior goes into battle without being prepared. List the elements of the Armor given to us by God for our equipment, along with any thoughts you have.

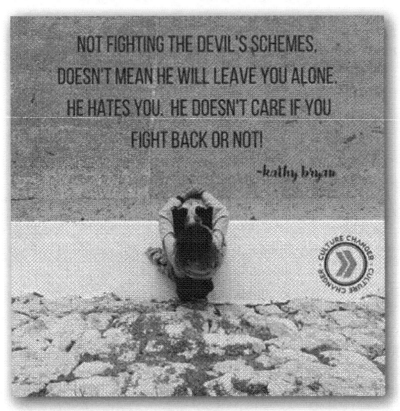

Roadmap to Redemption Chapter 7 Questions

1. "Truth Statements" are powerful and necessary weapons. Do you have any favorite(s)?

_____

_____

_____

_____

_____

_____

_____

_____
_____
_____

2. Read the following and note any experiences or thoughts on this passage below.

Many of us love to praise Him. Was it a new thought for you to use praise as a weapon? Psalm 22:3 teaches us that God inhabits the praises of His people. So, true heartfelt praise not only brings us into His presence, it ushers in peace and joy. What better place to be when we feel the battle, than in the presence of our God? What better weapon could we have? The darkest, bleakest moments of this life can be brightened and joy-filled when praises are sung. There is no greater strength than the Lord. Satan and his demons will flee from praise. More than anything satan wants to be worshipped. The last place he wants to be is surrounded by words and songs praising God. Prayer may be our battle, but Praise is the victory! It's evident throughout scripture. Acts 16 tells how Silas and Paul, having been whipped and beaten were locked in chains and thrown in prison. Yet, they chose prayer and praise because there is no greater place than the presence of God.

It's important for us to remember to focus our fight on our true enemy. More often than not, it isn't flesh and blood we are fighting but the enemy and his schemes. The enemy loves to use people as pawns to create discord, drama, and isolation. This tactic reminds me of the manipulation used by traffickers.

_____
_____
_____
_____
_____
_____
_____
_____
_____
_____

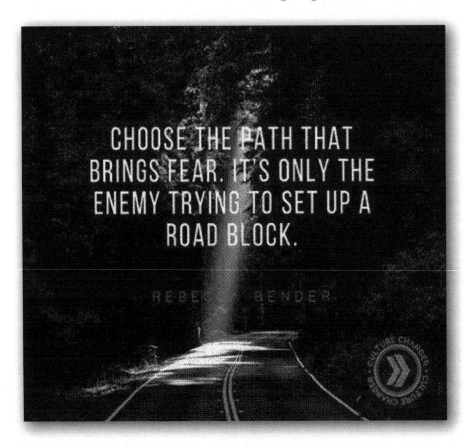

3. Always remember, go TOWARD the fear! What is satan trying to keep you away from?

_____
_____
_____
_____
_____
_____
_____
_____
_____
_____
_____

Ephesians 6:10-12 The Message

"And that about wraps it up. God is strong, and He wants you strong. So take everything the Master has set out for you, well-made weapons of the best materials. And put them to use so you will be able to stand up to everything the Devil throws your way. This is no afternoon athletic contest that we'll walk away from and forget about in a couple of hours. This is for keeps, a life-or-death fight to the finish against the Devil and all his angels."

- Discuss this and post one of your "aha" moments or a big takeaway from this lesson. Respond to at least two other posts.

_____
_____
_____
_____
_____
_____
_____
_____
_____
_____
_____

MODULE SIX

Triggers

Read: Roadmap to Redemption, Chapter Eight

TACKLING TRIGGERS. THESE little jewels are like landmines planted within the soil of our soul, and we never know exactly when they will explode. The good news is they don't have to stay buried, causing mayhem. We can take control and diffuse them all.

This can be one of the tougher chapters of the book. We've had folks who try to avoid it, just quickly perusing the material and moving on, rather than digging in. We've also had folks who camp out here, nearly getting stuck. I want to encourage you to try to avoid either of these reactions. Instead, look at the material, and take it in bite size chunks. Pray as you are going through it. God will give you the strength you need, if you depend on Him for it.

Digging up and neutralizing these triggers is an enormous step toward the deeper levels of freedom you haven't yet walked in but truly are awaiting you. You are brave! You can do this!

*PS: You won't address every trigger you will ever experience in this chapter. The **key** is to deal with each one as it comes, just like Rebecca did in the book (pg. 106). How? First, recognize these feelings you are experiencing are not from the current situation, get alone, ask God to reveal to you why you are feeling this way, and listen for the response, then once you know the cause, deal with it. It will be one of two things, a sin done to you or a sin committed by you. Either ask forgiveness, or give forgiveness, ask God to heal that part of your heart, and remove any root of bitterness.*

*We don't need nor deserve to be weighed down or held back by someone else's actions. Holding onto things, no matter how grievous, hurts us, not them. It is like drinking poison, and expecting it to hurt the other person. Let's choose not to give what they did any more power in our lives. Forgiving, is like releasing. It is **NOT** condoning, in any way. I fully know this can be a difficult concept to accept. But, I have found it to be true in my own life and healing, as has Rebecca.*

While we were being trafficked, we were used to pushing things down, stuffing our emotions. It was necessary to our survival. That is no longer true. So, when you experience a landmine, don't try to ignore it or allow that trigger to control you. Find a quiet spot and deal with it then. Dig it up and diffuse it, every time, so it can no longer torment you.

Roadmap to Redemption Chapter 8 Questions

Lessons we've learned throughout the book that help us with triggers:

- Thinking back to the last memory
- Asking, "Where were you, Jesus?"
- Replacing the lie with the truth
- Every time the thought resurfaces, taking it captive
- Reminding satan out loud of God's redemption

1. Which of these is your "go to" weapon? Do you have one we didn't discuss?

_____

_____

_____

2. Which of the Fruits of the Spirit do you need to work on the most?

_____

_____

_____

3. Which of the triggers Rebecca listed on pages 103-107 is your biggest challenge? Are there any that aren't listed?

- Money
- Anger
- Men
- Authority

- Impulsivity
- Memories
- Drama
- Control

You are not alone! You are not the only one dealing with triggers and feelings that are hard to understand. God knows full well the path to freedom after captivity can be very difficult. Difficult to the point we may be tempted to give up and return. Allowing ourselves the time and space and grace to heal is essential.

Just take a look at this scripture from Exodus. Moses was leading the Israelites from captivity in Egypt towards the Promised Land. Read Exodus 13:17 below, then read it again replacing Pharaoh's name with the person who exploited you, and the people with your name.

Exodus 13:17 NIV
*"When <u>Pharaoh [trafficker]</u> let the <u>people [you]</u> go, God did not lead them on the road through the Philistine country, though that was shorter. For God said, "If they [you] face war, they [you] might **change their minds and return** to Egypt."*

The Amplified Version says, *"Lest the people **change their purpose** when they see war and return to Egypt."* Change their minds also meant, *"to comfort oneself and flee."*

4. What are your thoughts after reading this?

_____

_____

_____

God wants to help you restore and rebuild your life. The enemy will use ANYTHING to get you distracted, to get you stressed, to get you anxious. While everything you have survived has made lasting impact, you can and will be able to thrive, and the enemy will continue to try and make you believe that you are not renewed and redeemed. Just remember, the enemy is a liar!

When we have been implanted with a dream from God, it needs time to develop. But, when it's ready, nothing will be able to stop it from coming forth. You can hold onto that promise!!!

Hebrews 6:19
"This confidence (assured belief) is like a strong and trustworthy anchor for our souls. It leads us through the curtain of heaven into God's inner sanctuary."

Drawing Near to God

Rewrite Ephesians Chapter Six in your own handwriting

DRAWING NEAR TO God includes walking in His ways, even when they don't make sense to us. This is definitely where trust comes in to play for many of us. Especially given the fact that we have been mistreated and hurt by the very people who were supposed to protect us.

As you copy Ephesians down, allow yourself to think on the verses and what they mean. Note the parts that don't seem to make sense to you. Ask God to give you deeper understanding. He says many times in scripture, ask me, seek understanding, seek wisdom. He is not a God who wants to keep us in the dark or always blindly following Him. There are times when we do not understand, and we are to follow anyway, but He does bring understanding to us, when we seek it, and seek more of Him.

Parts of this will be hard. That's ok. We will be discussing it. Remember, the scriptures were written to His children, not to the world. This passage is basically examples walking out the golden rule, "Love your neighbor as yourself." In fact, it reminds me of a necklace I have that is inscribed with, "Seek Justice, Love Mercy, Walk Humbly." It is taken from the book of Micah in the Old Testament.

> *But he's already made it plain how to live, what to do,*
> *what GOD is looking for in men and women.*
> *It's quite simple: Do what is fair and just to your neighbor,*
> *be compassionate and loyal in your love,*
> *and don't take yourself too seriously-*
> *take God seriously. Micah 6:8 (msg)*

From Kathy-

Before we start diving into Ephesians and all of the amazing edification God gives us to stay the course, to fight for your future and to walk with the Lord, I want to briefly touch on the issue of "slavery" since it comes up in this chapter of the Bible.

While the Bible doesn't overtly, in your face, condemn the practice of slavery, it does give instructions on how slaves should be treated. Those instructions can be found in Deuteronomy 15:12-15, Ephesians 6:9, and Colossians 4:1.

Now, because there is no one scripture that states slavery is an abomination, some people have taken that as evidence that God actually condones it. The thing is just like every other scripture it is important to read it in context, both textually and historically. In this time period, slavery was much different than what was practiced within the transatlantic slave trade, or elsewhere in the world in modern times. During biblical times, it tended to be based more on economics and social status, rather than race. For instance, Roman slaves, or bond-servants, either entered into slavery by selling themselves to compensate for debts they owed or to provide financially for their families, or they were spoils of war. Some actually chose it because they would have all their needs bet by the master. Slaves of that day were often well-educated, were treated with dignity, allowed to accumulate wealth, to marry, run businesses, and even purchase their own freedom. In fact, two-thirds of the Roman Empire were slaves, and Roman law normally set slaves free by the age of 30, if they hadn't been already.

The slavery that occurred in the United States is actually **condemned** in the Bible because it was based on race; fueled by the belief there was somehow an inferior race or human being. In Genesis 1:27, the Bible teaches us that ALL men are created by God, in His image. If this is the case, there can obviously not be an inferior race! In fact, the practice of "man-stealing" or kidnapping, is condemned in the both the Old and New Testaments and is abhorrent to God. This is exactly what occurred when the peoples of Africa were rounded up and stolen by slave hunters and traders, and brought to America. The penalty for this in the Bible under the Mosaic Law was death, as detailed in Exodus 21:16. In the NT, kidnappers are labeled "ungodly and sinful" and included in the same category as murderers, see 1 Timothy 1:8-10.

So basically, just like all the other sins, God is not "for" slavery, nor does He condone it. He does however, send us Jesus and give us the Bible, providing for our salvation. Experiencing God's amazing love, mercy, and grace creates change within us, restoring and redeeming us from the inside out. This changes how we think and act. So, rather than making a demand for society to reform itself, He provides the way for change to occur internally which causes a person to realize enslaving another is completely wrong.

Ephesians 6 (MSG)

6 **1-3** *Children, do what your parents tell you. This is only right. "Honor your father and mother" is the first commandment that has a promise attached to it, namely, "so you will live well and have a long life."*

⁴ Fathers, don't exasperate your children by coming down hard on them. Take them by the hand and lead them in the way of the Master.

⁵⁻⁸ Servants, respectfully obey your earthly masters but always with an eye to obeying the real master, Christ. Don't just do what you have to do to get by, but work heartily, as Christ's servants doing what God wants you to do. And work with a smile on your face, always keeping in mind that no matter who happens to be giving the orders, you're really serving God. Good work will get you good pay from the Master, regardless of whether you are slave or free.

⁹ Masters, it's the same with you. No abuse, please, and no threats. You and your servants are both under the same Master in heaven. He makes no distinction between you and them.

A Fight to the Finish

¹⁰⁻¹² And that about wraps it up. God is strong, and he wants you strong. So take everything the Master has set out for you, well-made weapons of the best materials. And put them to use so you will be able to stand up to everything the Devil throws your way. This is no afternoon athletic contest that we'll walk away from and forget about in a couple of hours. This is for keeps, a life-or-death fight to the finish against the Devil and all his angels.

¹³⁻¹⁸ Be prepared. You're up against far more than you can handle on your own. Take all the help you can get, every weapon God has issued, so that when it's all over but the shouting you'll still be on your feet. Truth, righteousness, peace, faith, and salvation are more than words. Learn how to apply them. You'll need them throughout your life. God's Word is an indispensable weapon. In the same way, prayer is essential in this ongoing warfare. Pray hard and long. Pray for your brothers and sisters. Keep your eyes open. Keep each other's spirits up so that no one falls behind or drops out.

¹⁹⁻²⁰ And don't forget to pray for me. Pray that I'll know what to say and have the courage to say it at the right time, telling the mystery to one and all, the Message that I, jailbird preacher that I am, am responsible for getting out.

²¹⁻²² Tychicus, my good friend here, will tell you what I'm doing and how things are going with me. He is certainly a dependable servant of the Master! I've sent him not only to tell you about us but to cheer you on in your faith.

²³⁻²⁴ Good-bye, friends. Love mixed with faith be yours from God the Father and from the Master, Jesus Christ. Pure grace and nothing but grace be with all who love our Master, Jesus Christ.

Ephesians 6 Questions

1. How did writing out Ephesians 6 help you? What insights did you have? What questions did it bring?

_____
_____
_____
_____
_____
_____
_____
_____
_____
_____

Drawing near to God

- Trusting Him
- Talking to Him
- Who is man?

Jeremiah 12:5 NLT - The Lord asks Jeremiah:
"If racing against mere man makes you tired, how will you race against horses? If you stumble and fall on open ground, what will you do in the thickets near the Jordan?"

"Not everyone who says to me, 'Lord, Lord,' will enter the kingdom of heaven, but only the one who does the will of my Father who is in heaven. Many will say to me on that day, 'Lord,
    Lord, did we not prophesy in your name and in your name drive out demons and in your name perform many miracles?' Then I will tell them plainly, 'I never knew you. Away from me, you evildoers!' " Matthew 7:21-23

The word "knew" in Greek is **ginosko.** It is the Jewish idiom for sexual intercourse between a man and a woman. It speaks of intimacy. God is saying, "You've said or done a lot of things: groups, bible studies, classes, Sunday service, home group, but do you *know* me? Are you intimate with me?" That is a question only you would know the answer to.

God desires a relationship with you. You are precious to Him. He wants to be intimate, like a husband and wife. There is nothing equal to being fully known, and fully accepted. Therein lies true intimacy.

2. Fill in these blanks:

My fears are_____

My dreams are _____

Although the omniscient Lord and Savior Jesus Christ knows it all, He desires conversations and relationships with us.

Points to Ponder

- Learning to talk with God builds that relationship
  - There are three voices: mine, His and the enemy's
  - The more you talk with Him, the more you get to know His voice.
- What kind of relationship would it be without mutual conversation?

Reminder, continue to work on your dream boards.
Achieving those dreams will require setting goals.

ACTIVITY: Read "Five Reasons Why You Should Commit Your Goals To Writing" by Michael Hyatt

https://michaelhyatt.com/5-reasons-why-you-should-commit-your-goals-to-writing.html

MODULE EIGHT

Positioning Yourself for Revelation

Read Roadmap to Redemption Chapters Nine and Ten

DEAR FRIEND! YOU have completed Roadmap to Redemption, and you are halfway through Elevate! We had no doubt that you would do well, and hope it has been an insightful and rewarding journey. This week we want to talk about 'normal.' What is it? What does it look like? Is it something we even want?

For a very long time in my life, I actually took pride in not being normal. I was glad to label myself as 'weird.' I think in some way it made me feel ok with the feeling that I didn't fit in. The vast majority of my life was spent feeling like I was on the outside looking in. I say all of this to say, I totally get it if you are thinking right now, "Normal? Who in the heck wants normal?"

Oftentimes, normal is equated with a Norman Rockwell painting, or a "Leave it to Beaver" style of family, or conforming to a standard set by others. Many survivors view 'normal' as how a bunch of 'squares,' who don't know the first thing about abuse, abandonment or the dark side of life, say to live. Others view it as the home of their childhood. Still others view it as this unattainable expectation they can never live up to. But….

The neat thing is, YOU get to decide what normal is to you. One of my favorite things about the healing process is feeling free to choose everything! I can choose what I want my life to look like. Now, we are the designers of our lives, after having been reduced to living how others dictated, it's finally our turn.

Remember, God can work with whatever situation you are currently in. It's you and Him. A team effort building your life, discovering yourself, looking to the future, as you learn, grow, heal and develop into the person you were created to be.

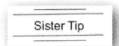 *Things to remember along the journey...*

- *"God has you right where He wants you! He can work with whatever situation you are in."*
- *It's just as important to forgive yourself, as it is anyone else.*

- *Keeping a "Discovering Me" journal is a great way to learn who you are. It can be an actual journal, or a pinterest board, or photo album. Every time I saw something I liked or was drawn to, I would paste a picture or brief explanation into my journal. It's neat to see how it develops.*
- *"I want a life I don't have to escape from." ~Chanel Toleston, graduate*
- *"My compassion wasn't complete because, it didn't include me." ~Brooke Axtell*

Roadmap to Redemption Chapter Nine Questions

1. Normalcy? What does it look like? Do we want it? How do we get it?

_____
_____
_____
_____
_____
_____
_____
_____
_____
_____
_____

2. What in this chapter stood out the most?

_____
_____
_____
_____
_____
_____
_____
_____
_____
_____

Roadmap to Redemption Chapter Ten Questions

1. What revelations have you had just within the last seven modules of this course?

_____
_____

_____
_____
_____
_____
_____
_____
_____
_____
_____

2. After reading this chapter, have you noticed any changes in the way you think toward circumstances that arise? In what ways?

_____
_____
_____
_____
_____
_____
_____
_____
_____
_____

3. What are some other questions, besides these two, we can ask ourselves to position ourselves for revelation?

- Lord, what are you trying to teach ME through this?
- What can I do differently next time?

_____
_____
_____
_____
_____
_____
_____
_____
_____
_____

Rebecca gave a great example of partnering with rage. There are many other things we can partner with: isolation, withdrawal, etc.   We'd like to challenge you not to skim over this part. Really dig in and find out what it is and be rid of it!

4. Has there been a time, or numerous times, when you felt yourself being EXTREME?

Knowing that extreme is not healthy what steps have you done from Chapter 10 to seek what you have partnered with throughout your life?

_____
_____
_____
_____
_____
_____
_____
_____
_____
_____
_____

Sister Tip

Points to Ponder

- *What does "revelation" even mean? How do we get more Paradigm Shifts, think differently, etc.?*
- *Am I always looking for an "ah ha" moment?*
- *"What could I have done differently? How can this help my future?" Find YOUR part in every situation.*

Hopefully you have enjoyed creating your dream board. Submit your completed project to your mentor by the end of the module.

HOMEWORK: Take these assessments, recording your results, and read "First Impressions Tips," found in Module 9.

Personality   https://www.16personalities.com/free-personality-test
Learning   http://www.educationplanner.org/students/self-assessments/learning-styles-quiz.shtml
Careers   http://www.personalitypage.com/html/careers.htm

PHASE TWO

Professional and Business

MODULE NINE

First Impressions

WELCOME TO MODULE Nine. If you haven't already done so, stop now and go take the assessments listed at the end of module eight, writing down your results. You may be wondering what your personality type has to do with making a great first impression. Actually, you will find it very helpful.

You see, knowing yourself well is a very important ingredient in first impressions. Whether you have a problem with self-esteem and confidence, or not. It's also vital to understand what *kind* of first impression you make. We all want to be seen for who we really are. But, there may be things you do or say that cause you to be misunderstood.

For example, even someone who is really confident in themselves may experience anxiety meeting new people. When we are anxious, our body language and the way we communicate is different, because we aren't feeling ourselves. This could very well cause the first impression to be less positive, simply because the impression is made with limited and false information. Similarly, a person who is naturally shy, may be viewed as aloof or arrogant by someone they are meeting for the first time, when in fact, they are a warm, caring, modest individual.

Ultimately, the more we know about ourselves and our personal idiosyncrasies, the more confident we will feel during these situations. We do want to caution you not to look at this as a search for what's wrong. Rather, it's a quest to find out how to be the best you possible. Learning about these things gives us the ability to tweak, and adjust anything we can, so we feel we are putting our best foot forward, and an accurate depiction of who we really are. There is much peace and freedom found in that. And may actually bring you more self-confidence in personal interactions with others.

First Impressions Questions

1. **Know** Yourself: Discuss your results from the personality and learning style assessments.

_____

_____

_____

_____

_____

2. Know your Audience: How you can use your test results to make a good impression?

_____

_____

_____

_____

_____

Personal appearance matters. It is an outward expression of ourselves and one that many take very seriously. Using clothing, makeup, and accessories to convey more about ourselves can be very enjoyable. While there is nothing wrong with this at all, we should always take into consideration the venue. Just like we wouldn't expect to see someone sporting an itsy, bitsy, teeny, weeny, yellow polka-dot bikini at the annual gala, we really don't expect to see torn jeans and a sweatshirt on the receptionist. These outfits are appropriate in different environs.

So, what am I saying? Just like we have a perfect outfit for a night on the town, we need to have attire that is perfect for the professional side of our lives. When choosing our professional wardrobe, we need to consider impression we are trying to convey. It's really no different than a uniform. We totally expect a policeman to wear a uniform. We do not expect, and would most likely not be filled with confidence if the officer responding to our need is dressed in bell bottoms and a floral button down shirt.

Clothing and hygiene definitely convey a strong message. What message do we want to send? Professionally, a look that conveys strength, confidence, and approachability, among others, is a great place to start. It should never be distracting. In the business arena, we want to be known for what we can do with our brain and our talents, not how sexy, trendy or hip we are.

3. Check your Appearance (hair, makeup, jewelry, clothing): What changes are you ready to make? Keep your objective in mind!

_____

_____

_____

_____

_____

First Impressions - tips

1. **Eye contact**

    Making eye contact when getting to know someone is essential. People who make good eye contact are often considered trustworthy, confident, open and integrous. If this is a difficult prospect for you, remember, simply looking at their eyes long enough to note their eye color, and say 'great' is long enough. It will usually result in you smiling, which has the added benefit of placing you in a good mood. Eye contact is a skill you can cultivate.

2. **Building Rapport**

    Paying attention to a new acquaintance's gestures, rate of speech, posture, and body language and adjusting yours to theirs is a critical component in building rapport. There are a few keys though. To avoid seemingly mocking the person, you want to be sure you are truly listening and engaged. Then, mirroring their stance, and gestures will usually have the other person relaxed and at ease with you. Also, try to match your rate of speech to that of theirs. Basically, we like people who imitate us….if we don't realize they are doing it.

3. **Slaying Anxiety**

    Simply worrying about making a good first impression can be enough to make anxiety levels sky-rocket. Seeming anxious doesn't make for a great start. So, what do you do? DO be yourself! Trying to be something you're not, will only increase your anxiety. DO control your breathing and rate of speech. Anxious people tend to talk really quickly. DO nix the fidgeting. If you can't help fidgeting, try channeling all of that energy into one silent object you can hold in your hand, like a rubber band, worry stone or paper clip. DO disguise a bad mood. Your friends would know this was not the normal you, but a new acquaintance may think you are a Debbie-downer, plus, bad moods are contagious. A genuine smile will help lift your mood, and present them with your best face.

4. **The Art of Conversation**

    Let's face it, we all like to talk about ourselves, even when we think we don't! When interacting with people, especially someone new, focus on them. Keep the question, "How am I making them feel?" in mind. The idea is to get to know them better, not share all of our glorious endeav-ors. Listen intently. Respond genuinely. Ask questions. Resist the urge to interrupt and "one up" what they've shared. Humans like to know they are being listened to, which will garner you much respect and appreciation. These tips will leave you feeling like you know them better, and leave them feeling they've made a great new contact.

5. **One more time**

    We've all had the moment when we opened our mouth and inserted both feet, brushed some-one off, or just overlooked someone, completely making a bad first impression. When you find yourself in this situation, take a deep breath, and go back to the person and use humor or a bit of humility, to build a bridge. For example, you might say, "I see you have meet my evil twin." Or, "I'm sorry I wasn't myself earlier." Most people are gracious, and can totally relate to having an off moment.

6. **Compliments**

When used sparingly, flattery is a terrific tool to win people, or even to break the ice. Several years ago I noticed just how much I thought nice things about people, but didn't mention them. So, I made a decision to try as much as possible to say the nice things I was thinking. It has been a great decision. We all enjoy a nice compliment, just as long as it's sincere. We don't want to be phony, we do want to be encouraging.

7. **Clothes Sense**

It's been said clothes make the man. Well, they definitely leave an impression, and you want that to be a great impression. Professional, yet understated is what you are going for. Short skirts, tight bodices, cleavage, jeans with holes, sports gear are all no-no's.

Instead, build a business wardrobe of neat, professional pieces that you can mix and match. You can find great buys at department store sales, nicer consignment, or thrift stores, etc. You do not need to spend a lot, but you do need a business quality wardrobe. Dressing profession-ally will also help you feel more confident and prepared.

Keep your makeup basic, clean and professional, as well, but not overdone. A 2011 study in PLoS One revealed people thought women who wore makeup were more likable, competent and trustworthy than women who didn't wear makeup. Beware, that too much makeup will to-tally kill a first impression.

Email, Computer Skills & Writing Tips

Email

IN TODAY'S ELECTRONIC world, using email communication a given. Professionalism within your email is a must, whether you are job seeking, conversing with a co-worker or a client. Remembering your email is an extension of you and your business may help you take the extra effort to make each one the best. This does not take a lot of time, it does take some consideration of a few things that we will cover here.

1. **Proofread:** Once you hit send anyone can read it simply because of the ability to forward. So make sure you wouldn't mind that note being seen in the headlines. Proofread your email, both for typos and spelling errors. Another hint, waiting to enter the email address until after all of the above is complete prevents it from being sent before you are ready.

2. **Signature:** It is quick and easy to set up your email signature one time, and it will then be included on each and every email. Include all of the contact information you want people to have access to within your signature, such as, your title, company name, social media, and website address. Do the same with your mobile phone. It is much better than having the tagline "send from my iPhone" on the bottom of your correspondence.

3. **Templates:** If you have certain types of emails you receive frequently, simply save a pre-written response in your drafts folder and then copy, paste, and tweak for that specific response. Done!

4. **Bullet Points:** People tend to scan emails, rather than read them. Good or bad, you help avoid email roulette by utilizing bullet points to list the important items and steps in the email. Just like you want your questions answered, be careful when replying to emails that you respond to all questions asked of you.

5. **Tone:** When you read something written by your mom you can hear 'her' voice in your head as you read. Because you know her so well, you literally hear the tone of her voice. Conversely, we don't always know the people we are emailing. Therefore, it's important to compose your communication in such a way the tone is understood. You don't want to sound cold, but you also don't want to sound too familiar or casual. Similarly, if the issue is

particularly sensitive, you may consider picking up the phone and discussing it, since nuance is not easily conveyed via email.

Computer Tips & Shortcuts

I don't know about you but, I love streamlining processes and timesavers. There are keyboard shortcuts that are easily memorized, and have you shaving time one keystroke after the next. Seriously, they are much faster than a touchpad or mouse. Below are a few, and we have a complete list in the Activities section of the Elevate Academy. Give them a try!

CTRL+A: Select All   CTRL+C: Copy
CTRL+X: Cut   CTRL+V: Paste
CTRL+Z: Undo   CTRL+Y: Redo
CTRL+B: Bold   CTRL+U: Underline
CTRL+I: Italic   CTRL+P: Print
CTRL+F: Find   ALT+Tab: scrolls thru open windows
ALT+F4: closes active window   WIN+E: open file explorer
WIN+P: projector settings   WIN+D: minimize all to the desktop
WIN+L: lock   CTRL+I: Italic

Writing Tips

Communicating with the written word cannot be avoided. Putting your best foot forward means using proper grammar, correct spelling, and a rich vocabulary. All of us don't have these things naturally, but we can practice, and learn to put them into place. Below you will find a chart of commonly misused words.

YOU'RE	YOU ARE
YOUR	IT BELONGS TO YOU
THEY'RE	THEY ARE
THEIR	IT BELONGS TO THEM
THERE	A PLACE
WE'RE	WE ARE
WERE	PAST TENSE OF ARE (we were at store)

WHERE	A PLACE
THEN	A POINT IN TIME
THAN	A METHOD OF COMPARING
TWO	THE NUMBER 2
TO	INDICATES MOTION
TOO	ALSO OR EXCESSIVELY, ADDITIONALLY

1. Wordsmithing: Avoid word repetition by using a thesaurus to find a suitable synonym. Remember though, all synonyms are not created equal and do not have the exact meaning or use. Often, the words are indeed similar, but used quite differently and in different contexts. If you don't know how to use a word properly, don't use it. You do not want the attempt to improve your writing backfiring on you. For example, stumble, fall, and backslide are synonyms, but in this sentence interchanging them changes the connotation of the sentence. *That was quite a stumble. That was quite a fall. That was quite a backslide.*

    A second reason to use a thesaurus is to find replacements for common or boring words. Here are some examples:

    > Purchase = buy
    > That = describe the thing which you are speaking of
    > Discard = throw away
    > Locations = places
    > Believe = think

2. Take it to the next level by increasing your vocabulary and news topics knowledge. Many people feel they don't have a terrific, diverse vocabulary. Expanding your knowledge and use of words enables you to communicate in an even more clear and concise way.

A few ways to easily expand your vocabulary are:

- Read! Seriously, the more you read, the more words you will be exposed to. As you come to unknown words, the context may explain the meaning, but also look them up in the dictionary.
- Commit to learn a word a day. There are both calendars and apps that assist with this.
- Jot new words down in a journal or list. It will help you remember them, and encourage you in your endeavor to expand your vocabulary

Below are a few words to get you started:

- Gregarious
- Genuflect
- Trepidation
- Vetted
- Interpersonal

Activity: Compose one paragraph using the five new vocabulary words and post it in the community.

MODULE ELEVEN

Work Ethic

HAVING A STRONG work ethic is vital to a company achieving its goals. While that is true, you don't often hear it pointed out that a strong work ethic is also vital to you, personally, achieving your goals. The things we want to accomplish in this life will not just happen. It is up to us to do our part to make the dreams God has planted within us, come to fruition.

Work ethic is not just a list of great qualities. At its core, a strong work ethic values people, morals, and doing the right thing in situations that arise.   Let's take a look at a few examples.

- **Punctuality**- 10 minutes early IS on time.
  - Arriving on time displays honor for others, yourself and the task before you
- **Serving**- The last shall be first. Serve someone else's vision.
  - Serving? Aren't we supposed to be learning how to achieve our dreams? Yes! Just like nearly all of God's precepts, this seems upside down to us. Serving another's dream will also serve your own! Look through the Bible. Every leader served another before they were called to lead. Great leaders are servants with a mission. Jesus is the best servant of all, with the biggest mission of all. We don't need a much better example, now do we?
- **Notes-** NEVER go to a meeting without the ability to take notes.
  - This is part of being prepared. Keep a small notepad and pen with you. Can't write fast enough or writing is illegible? Fine, no excuses! Use the recording app on your phone to take notes, or type them into a note-taking app.
- **Interviews-** Interviews begin in the parking lot.
  - So, don't pick nose, pull your underwear out of your butt, etc. Seriously, you never know if the person interviewing you has a window overlooking the parking lot.
  - Prep for your interview briefly researching the company. Learn what they are about, how long they've been in existence, etc. Know which position you are applying for, and some of the qualities that make you the perfect fit.
  - Bring the proper documentation, ID, your resume, references, and something to take notes with.

"Whatever you do, do your work heartily, as for the Lord rather than for men." Colossians 3:23
NASB

"And whatever you do or say, do it as a representative of the Lord Jesus, giving thanks through him to God the Father." Colossians 3:17 NIV

"Work with enthusiasm, as though you were working for the Lord rather than for people." Ephesians 6:7 NIV

- **Honesty**
  Honesty. We all know that means to tell the truth. So what does that have to do with work ethic? It's actually the cornerstone of good work ethic. Being honest is not simply being true to your word, but in your actions and behavior, as well. Not using company time to check your social media, write personal emails, or do your nails are examples of honesty in the workplace, as is not using work supplies for personal reasons. Lastly, honesty creates open communication that is important in any work situation.

- **Personal Integrity**
  Someone with personal integrity displays ethical and moral principles, both in the workplace and in their personal life. Their word can be trusted, deadlines will be met, and mistakes will be owned rather than excuses offered. They understand right from wrong and show that in all they do.

- **Responsibility**
  A responsible person takes ownership of their work, puts in their best effort and takes their job seriously. They can be depended upon to do what is expected without being reminded or monitored. No matter what happens, they can be trusted to respond appropriately in any situation, including taking responsibility for their own mistakes, and asking for what they need to proper execute their duties.

- **Optimism**
  This quality may not have been on your radar of characteristics that comprise good work ethic. However, a positive outlook leads to many other things, such as noticing the talents in others, resisting negative reactions when things don't go as planned, continuing to look for alternative strategies when one way doesn't work out. This trait is one sought out by employers. Seriously, who wants to hang out with a habitual naysayer?

- **Self-Motivated**
  Whether you work for yourself or an employer, self-motivation is an essential quality to have. Being able to complete the tasks at hand on time, and without someone looking over your shoulder displays responsibility and trustworthiness. A self-motivated person is able to hold themselves accountable, stay organized and inspired to get the job done.

- **Team Player**

  Someone with a good work ethic has the ability to be a team player. At some point, you will find yourself on a team. Being a part of a team can be rewarding, and it can also be challenging. How well you interact with others on the team, can determine the outcome of the project.

  You've probably heard it said, "No man is an island!" Even if you prefer to work alone, the truth is no one is great at everything. Teams can truly make a project richer and much easier to complete, but only when we honor each other and the talents each member brings to the table. Basically, learning to focus on what is best for the project and leveraging each individual's talents, rather than ourselves.

Work Ethics Questions

1. Which of these areas do you feel you need to work on the most?

   _____

   _____

   _____

   _____

   _____

2. What can you do to begin improving in those areas?

   _____

   _____

   _____

   _____

   _____

> **Sister Tip**
>
> *Perfectionism and being a workaholic are not great 'faults." They are not strengths disguised as weakness. Here's a terrific article explaining why:*

https://www.themuse.com/advice/5-reasons-being-a-perfectionist-actually-is-your-biggest-weakness-and-not-just-in-interviews

MODULE TWELVE

Sensationalism, Re-exploitation & Media

Sensationalism
WHAT IS IT? What can we do about it? Why do we care?

Sensationalism- noun; subject matter, language, or style producing or designed to produce startling or thrilling impressions or to excite and please vulgar taste.

Well, after reading the definition, hopefully we will know both what it is and why we don't want it. But, what can we do about it? Obviously, we cannot control other people's actions, however, we can control ours and our reactions to things we consider unwanted.

Sensationalism, particularly in the arena of discussing, educating, and bringing awareness to human trafficking is definitely unwanted at best and inflammatory at worst. In fact, in an attempt to sensationalize or startle, sensationalizing a survivor's experience can often border on exaggeration, which we all know is a form of untruth. The last thing we need to aid the human trafficking movement is untruth. We need truth in education, in whatever form that takes: article, blog, personal story, training, PSA, etc.

So, we can choose in all of our own communications to be factual. We can determine to notice sensationalism and educate the authors of such.

Sensationalism can also be seen in the media with images that show an unrealistic depiction of the reality of sexual exploitation. These types of images fuel the very misperceptions that we as advocates try really hard to break. Mainstream media has taken a couple images that are actually harmful to the movement. If invited to an event where one of these images is used for advertising, gently ask if the imaging can be changed to fit something more realistic. Consider asking to view and approve advertising prior to print to ensure accuracy. More importantly, ensure, as leaders, that we stay accountable to represent accuracy within the movement.

1. Consider this information and list a few instances of what you would consider sensationalism.

_____

_____

_____

_____

_____

2. If you have ever used material or explanations that you'd now consider to be sensational, how can you reword, or retool them to more appropriately educate on HT in America?

_____

_____

_____

_____

_____

Re-Exploitation
What is it and how can I protect myself from it?

Exploitation- noun; the action or fact of treating someone unfairly in order to benefit from their work; capitalizing upon

Survivors of human trafficking have already been exploited. Unfortunately, it is not uncommon for them to be re-exploited by people or organizations that want to 'use' them for their story, while not recognizing them for their other strengths or properly compensating them for their time, as you would other professionals.

The best way to avoid this from happening to you is to be aware it's possible and to know how to represent yourself.

How do you represent yourself? Ensure you have an MOU (Memorandum of Understanding) or job description that does a great job setting clear expectations. Make sure your compensation is comparable to industry standard.

Consider this: Traffickers have asked you to share intimate parts of yourself in order for them to make money. If organizations ask you to share intimate parts of yourself so they can make money, then clearly there are too many parallels.

Questions to consider:

- Am I being compensated the same as everyone else. (If everyone is missionary status or volunteer, and they are asking you to be also, that is not re-exploitation)
- Am I being treated as a professional with my thoughts, points and concerns being heard and treated as valuable?
- Are there opportunities for leadership positions?

3. Do you feel you have been in a re-exploitive situation?

_____
_____
_____
_____
_____

4. If so, in retrospect, would this information have aided in preventing that situation, or at least made you feel more equipped?

_____
_____
_____
_____
_____

Tokenism

We all know what the phrase "token black man" or in some cases, "token white guy" means. Being a survivor can often be no different. Is an organization simply inviting you to be their token survivor, or are they actually allowing you to have a voice, a decision-making space? Are they allowing and encouraging you to get training and to be empowered? Being empowered would mean allowing you to find the talents and abilities that you have and come alongside to help you develop them.

Media: Tips and questions to consider

The prospect of dealing with the media, whether it's print, radio or tv is daunting for some, and downright scary for others. Thankfully, it doesn't have to be that way. With a little preparation, and introspection you can feel confident and more than capable to not only handle these situations, but make them beneficial.

Start by reviewing these:

- **Is it helpful to you?**
  - You don't "owe" it to anyone to do an interview, presentation, or share your story
  - Is it something you want to do because you personally see the value in it?
- **Is it what you want?**
  - Ask yourself, if no one else wanted you to, would you still want to, and be ok with sharing your story, doing the interview or presentation?
- **Could it hurt you or your family?**
  - Are you at a place in life where publicity will not harm you?
- **Are you ready?**
  - Have you shared this before?
  - Do you feel your healing has progressed to the point this won't be traumatizing?
  - Does your advocate concur with that assessment?
- **Ask yourself these questions:**
  - Is there any part of your past that you are ashamed of?
  - Is there any part of your present that you are ashamed of?
  - Is there anything that you don't want your family knowing?
  - If you were recognized and approached in public, how would you feel?
- **You are going for it… now what?**
  - Consider having an advocate or support person with you; most survivors won't be without one…even after they've been doing this a long time. It's easier to have someone advocate for you, than doing it yourself.
- **Prepare ahead of time** how you will handle any questions you do not want to answer or questions that are particularly difficult, by having a 'stock answer.' Never say, "No comment."
  - Ex: "I'm fairly sure everyone can imagine the danger, hurt, pain, degradation, intense trauma that comes from being raped daily, however, I feel people would be best served by knowing…"
  - Ex: "No, I am sorry, but I am not comfortable speaking about that at this time." Or, when they say something like, "I know you said you didn't want to go in to detail, but…" You can reply with, "Yes, you are right, I do not want to go into detail. I do not feel it is appropriate nor safe for me to go into that at this time."
  - Ex: "I can understand why one would ask that question, but I strongly feel people would be better served knowing…"
- **Request**, in advance, and/or what the purpose/theme of the story will be, and what questions will be asked

- **Practice** beforehand
- **Have info** you want to share prepared to give them. A few examples, your website, contact info, a bit about what you do now/who you work with, etc.
- **Always** ask to Fact Check the finished piece. This is not editing nor approving the article as a whole, it is simply checking the facts you provided for accuracy.
- **Take the time** while with the interviewer to educate on the proper terms to use. Or send a language handout prior to the interview. Ex: prostituted, not prostitute; exploited child, not child prostitute; etc. (See the handout at the end of this module's lesson, "How Language Shapes Our Perception")
- **Compensation** - I find this a good test: if you would expect someone else to receive payment for what you are doing, or if they are receiving payment, then you should also. (This usually ONLY applies to presenting, but I wanted to include it.)
- **Don't go** "off the record!" Pretend this phrase doesn't even exist.
- **Remember**, reporters only report as well as they take notes. Ask them to re-read that quote you just gave or if they had any questions they wanted clarity prior to you leaving.

Redirect

I've heard this called bridging, deflecting, and others, but I call it redirecting the question to be what you want it be about it.

We often can get asked questions that we may be uncomfortable with. However, without being completely rude, you can redirect the question back to a point YOU want to make. So think about your "niche" (which we'll dive into next module a little more), or think of a presentation you may have given recently. What were some of the points you made or make at presentations?

List 2-3 objectives that you want people to know about this issue. For example, mine are: 1) that trafficking in America looks very different than it does in a 3rd world country and 2) Sensationalism fuels misidentification. Now you try:

_____

_____

_____

_____

_____

Now anytime someone asks you a question that you are not comfortable with, redirect it to one of the points above. Let's try some.

Q: How many times were you raped a night?
A: Unfortunately, violence towards women is inevitable in this "industry" but what we all need to remember is (insert your point).

Q: How are your children now?
A: Children can be effected greatly by being involved in this crime, but what's important is (insert point).

Let's try a few more together. Write an example of a question you've been asked that you are not comfortable answering. Then see if you can redirect it to one of the points you listed above.

Q: _____
_____

A: _____
_____

Reflect on any interviews you have done. Note how you *would have* done any part of them differently now that you know some more tips. If you haven't yet interacted with media, take some time now to consider what and how you would like that to happen.

Activity: Practice Q&A with a friend, mentor or in your group

HOMEWORK: Watch Amy Cuddy's TED Talk prior to the next meeting. http://www.ted.com/talks/amy_cuddy_your_body_language_shapes_who_you_are

HAND OUT FROM SHARED HOPE INTERNATIONAL THAT WE PROVIDE TO ALL MEDIA PRIOR TO TAKING AN INTERVIEW:

How Language Shapes Our Perception

Child Prostitute

- Insult/Derogatory Term
- Supports myths and misconceptions about prostitution
- A bad kid that has made poor choices

- Places blame on person rather than recognizing the organized crime structure
- Establishes a criminal justice response rather than victim/abuse response

Victims of Sex Trafficking

- Defines what has happened to the child, rather than labeling the child
- Indicates that there are multiple factors, persons and systems involved in the crime
- Recognizes a child cannot developmentally, socially, or legally make a "choice" in commercial sex
- Identifies that a perpetrator exists and calls for a criminal response for that perpetrator
- Identifies a victim and a person in need of support and services

Improper Term	Correct Term
Child Prostitute	Prostituted Child
Hooker	Victim of Exploitation
Teen Prostitute	Trafficked Teen, Exploited Youth
Pimp (often replaced with 'cool')	Trafficker
John/Trick	Purchaser of Sex, Buyer

*Elizabeth Scaife © Shared Hope International

MODULE THIRTEEN

Interpersonal Communication & Networking

Watch: Amy Cuddy **http://www.ted.com/talks/amy_cuddy_your_body_language_shapes_who_ you_are**

IN THIS MODULE we are discussing interpersonal communication. You can't have that discussion without talking a bit about body language. The truth is, much of our communication is done through non-verbal cues, not the spoken word. In fact, our bodies usually convey, more directly and honestly, what we are thinking than our words do.

So, what's the problem? Can't our bodies just say it all? Well, yes and no. We need to be aware of any bad habits we have regarding our body language. Once we recognize them, we can improve them, leading to more effective communication, which in turn leads to greater self-esteem and confidence, because we feel understood.

Here are two references with great examples of what non-verbal cues we need to remove. Read them over and honestly assess which apply to you.

http://www.marcandangel.com/2008/07/07/25-acts-of-body-language-to-avoid/
http://www.inc.com/peter-economy/9-body-language-habits-that-make-you-look-really-unpro-fessional.html

Interpersonal Communication Questions

1. Now, how about that Amy Cuddy? After hearing her research and findings, did you have any big takeaways?

_____

_____

_____

_____

2. Do you believe the premise our bodies can change our minds? Did you try any of the examples she gave? What did you discover?

_____

_____

_____

_____

_____

Great interpersonal communication is essentially determining to put your best foot forward. Here are some great tips, and the whys behind them.

- **Use eye contact to convey interest, attention, and honesty.**
  - Looking away, or down, or around the room is not good.
  - Making eye contact for a survivor can be super difficult.
  - To begin making this new habit, try looking on the forehead between the eyes or at the tip of the nose.
  - Practice making eye contact and holding it for several seconds. Doing this over time will help build a new habit of making and keeping good eye contact.
- **Use a handshake and a smile**
  - Use with introductions, whether personal or professional.
  - Convey warmth, strength, and confidence.
- **Talk about THEM**
  - Everyone likes to talk about himself or herself.
  - Asking questions about them conveys interest.
  - People tend to automatically "like" a person they just met who paid attention to them.
- **Network by getting and giving cards**
  - Always have your card with you.
  - Exchange them. If the other person doesn't offer, ask for it – it shows interest and helps them remember you.
  - The back of a card should be non-glossy, preferably white, making it great for identifying notes. Ex: "Friend of Rebecca, call to discuss speaking engagement."
- **Introvert? Pump yourself up**
  - Note-those power poses really work!
  - Introvert doesn't equal shy. Convey confidence and self-worth –SMILE, Smile, smile.
- **Use voice diction to control the conversation with just your voice**
  - The tone of your voice sets the tone. Be it objective, formal, emotional, distant, intimate, etc.

This is a lot of different information and tips to digest. It is all valuable! To avoid being overwhelmed, try implementing 2-3 tips at a time, moving on to the next 2-3 after those have become new habits.

ACTIVITY: Role Play in groups or with a friend

Interpersonal Work Skills

Interpersonal communication is a life skill in human behavior, feelings and attitudes. In order to make change in our attitudes and beliefs, it is necessary to focus on identifying and expressing feelings, recognizing and acknowledging specific behaviors and lastly, being responsible and accountable for one's own actions.

Interpersonal communication can be applied during personal problem solving. How often have you asked yourself *"Why,"* when you are presented with a problem, rather than "What can I do about this?" This way of thinking will provide you with an opportunity to learn new and helpful behaviors towards dealing with problems you may be facing.

Some important aspects of interpersonal skills are:

- Effectively translating and conveying information
- Being able to accurately interpret other people's emotions
- Being sensitive to other people's feelings
- Calmly arriving at resolutions to conflict
- Avoiding gossip

"For all that is secret will eventually be brought into the open, and everything that is concealed will be brought to light and made known to all." - Luke 8:17 NLT

3. What's your definition of gossip? What's God's definition? Do they match?

_____

_____

_____

_____

_____

4. Which of these work skills is the most challenging for you? Which do you excel at?

_____

_____

_____

_____

_____

If you think about it, many of these work skills are actually accomplished when we follow the golden rule found in Mathew 7:12. You know the one… *"Do unto others as you would have them do unto you."* Or as The Message translation says, [12] *"Here is a simple, rule-of-thumb guide for behavior: Ask yourself what you want people to do for you, then grab the initiative and do it for them. Add up God's Law and the Prophets and this is what you get."*

Homework: Read pages 5-17 from John Maxwell's *Developing the Leader Within You.*

PHASE THREE

Leadership

Leadership Defined: Influence

Read pages 5-17 from "Developing the Leader Within You"

Over the next three modules we will cover some crucial principles of leadership. We will be pulling some readings from John C. Maxwell's book, "Developing the Leader Within You." During this time, we highly encourage you to read the book in its entirety.

Leaders are influencers. Not rulers, nor dictators, though some leaders can make us feel otherwise. People say great leaders are born, but they are also created. Most importantly…YOU can become one!

Everyone has differing idea of what a leader is and should be. If we take all of the notions, ideas and moral issues away and look at the core, it's easy to see that a leader is simply someone who has the ability to acquire followers. Their ability to influence draws others to follow them. Each of us has been influenced by people in our lives, just as we have influenced others, whether we knew it or not. Because of the principle and power influence has, it's our responsibility to use that influence for good and to the best of our ability.

Influence grows stronger and more impactful when the leadership exudes genuine caring and concern for people. The bedrock of influence is effective communication. Which in itself is people-driven. Effective communication looks like coaching your team, encouraging them, making sure everyone is on the same page, and has the tools they need to complete the job. It explains why a mishap occurred, and how best to fix it, without playing the blame game. It exemplifies the truth that everything we do, no matter what our business is, comes back to people. People are the most important "why" of what anyone does and they are also our greatest assets.

1. Stop and jot down where your current areas of influence are, and who they affect. You may be surprised at what you find.

   _____

   _____

   _____

   _____

   _____

In this week's reading we learned about the levels of leadership, and the 'why' behind the people who follow a leader on each level. Let's review those now.

- Level One – **POSITION**: Here you are the leader because you were assigned the position. Basically, you have the 'right' to lead because of your title. At this level, people follow because they have to. Influence didn't make you a leader, at level one. But, your influence, and skills can take you from here to the next levels.

- Level Two – **PERMISSION**: Here you are the leader because you were given permission. You have the 'right' to lead because of your relationship with the person. At this level of leadership, you are intentionally building relationships by spending time and energy on their needs and goals. These people will choose to follow you because of the relationship, not because they have to. They have come to truly like you.

- Level Three – **PRODUCTION**: Here you are the leader because of what you have done within the organization. You have the 'right' to lead because what you've produced. At this level, people follow you because of the results. They have come to admire you. The momentum that has been created has people focused on accomplishing a purpose. You will still have relationship, but a results-oriented mindset has been achieved on the team.

- Level Four – **PEOPLE DEVELOPMENT**: Here you are the leader because of your ability to develop people. You have the 'right' to lead because of what you have done for them. At this level, people follow you because you empower them. They are loyal to you. Great leaders don't just lead, they raise up other great leaders. Success without a successor is failure.

- Level Five – **PERSONHOOD**: Here you are the leader because of who you are, and what you represent. Few leaders make it to this level, and only after many years spent developing people and growing organizations.

> Sister Tip
>
> *While this is referred to as levels of leadership, it's vital to remember a leader doesn't leave one level never to return. The preceding level must continue to be tended to as it supports the level above.*

- The higher you go, the greater the growth.
- You never leave the base level.
- If you are leading a group of people, you will not be on the same level with everyone.
- For your leadership to remain effective, it is essential that you take the other influencers within the group with you to the higher levels.

2. Remember question one? Where you listed your current circles of influence? Note what level of leadership you are on with those people you listed:

_____
_____
_____
_____

Great leaders have several essential qualities. They don't raise up followers, they raise up other leaders.

Great leaders are essentially people developers. Through empowering and serving them, leading with a good example, and continually building into them, they create great leaders. A successful leader always raises up a successor.

David is a good example of a great leader. He had his mighty men because he had the confidence and security in himself that allowed him to see the value and potential in the people around him. He learned what type of leader he DIDN'T want to be through his trials with King Saul. (1 Samuel 16 through 1 Kings 2)

3. What was something you underlined when reading the pages in "Developing the Leader Within" this module? What was something that impacted you? Why?

_____
_____
_____
_____
_____

Great leaders have great attitudes. Now would be the perfect time to review the teaching on attitudes from module four, on page 22.

Great leaders lead with compassion and humility. They are emotionally healthy, and do not allow emotion to control their decision making.

Great leaders never take the credit for work that someone else on the team did but publicly recognizes others.

Ingredients of Leadership

WE ALL HAVE things that just jump out at us when we think of our parents…good and bad, lol. One of those things for me is a true nugget of wisdom. My mom used to say, "A smart person learns from their mistakes, but a wise person learns from other people's mistakes." She was so very right about this! It is very unwise of us to only have a plan to learn from our own mistakes. Personally, I don't want to waste time learning things through my own experience that I could learn quicker, easier, and less painfully by heeding the actions of others.

There is so much wisdom to be had and so many techniques to employ as we learn and grow. If there were only one technique I hope you learn, though, it would be this one. Many of us, because of our experience, were shortchanged in the growing and developing department. Now, as adults, we are not only healing but oftentimes playing a strategic game of catch-up. So, please take this nugget to heart. It will serve you well.

Speaking of mistakes. Never, ever be afraid of making them. Why? When we are afraid of mistakes, we end up just warming the bench, instead of getting in the game. Being afraid of making mistakes keeps us from trying. When we don't try, it's then that we fail. You see, failure isn't making a mistake. Failure is not trying at all. Every time we try, we discover new things. It may be discovering how something doesn't work, but it's still valuable knowledge that will help on the next try. Remember, the greater the challenge, the more likely it is it will take several tries to accomplish. And the greater your need will be to have the ability to overcome and keep trying. If we never try, we will, indeed, NEVER succeed! Embrace trying! Keep learning and growing!

A great leader learns from mistakes by always being sure he owns them. So choose to completely avoid the blame game. We totally miss an opportunity for growth when we place blame elsewhere for our own mistake. Then, we end up making it again, because we didn't take ownership of it the first time. I hate going around and around the same mountain! Admitting them also has a secondary effect. Admitting it shows character and garners respect. Even when the mistake was something private and no one else knows of it, we still find respect for ourselves.

1. Do you pay enough attention to your mistakes to learn from them? What steps do you take to ensure not making them again?

_____

_____

_____

_____

_____

_____

_____

2. How do you define failure?

_____

_____

_____

_____

_____

_____

_____

Five Ingredients of Personal Growth by John C. Maxwell

"As any farmer knows, the growth of a crop only happens when the right ingredients are present. To harvest plentiful fields, the farmer has to begin by planting the right seed in rich topsoil where sunlight and water can help the seed to sprout, mature, and bear fruit. If any of the ingredients (seeds, topsoil, sunlight, or water) are missing, the crop won't grow.

Growing as a leader also requires the proper ingredients. Unless the right attitudes and actions are cultivated, an aspiring leader will sputter and fail rather than growing in influence. Let's look at five basic qualities essential for growth in leadership.

1) Teachability

Arrogance crowds out room for improvement. That's why humility is the starting point for personal growth. As Erwin G. Hall said, "An open mind is the beginning of self-discovery and growth. We can't learn anything new until we can admit that we don't already know everything."

Adopting a beginner's mindset helps you to be teachable. Beginners are aware that they don't know it all, and they proceed accordingly. As a general rule, they're open and humble, noticeably lacking in the rigidity that often accompanies experience and achievement. It's easy enough to have a beginner's mind when you're actually a beginner, but maintaining teachability gets trickier in the long term, especially when you've already achieved some degree of success.

2) Sacrifice

Growth as a leader involves temporary loss. It may mean giving up familiar but limiting patterns, safe but unrewarding work, values no longer believed in, or relationships that have lost their meaning.

Whatever the case, everything we gain in life comes as a result of sacrificing something else. We must give up to go up.

3) Security

To keep learning throughout life, you have to be willing, no matter what your position is, to say, 'Il don't know.' It can be hard for executives to admit lacking knowledge because they feel as if everyone is looking to them for direction, and they don't want to let down their people. However, followers aren't searching for perfection in their leaders. They're looking for an honest, authentic, and courageous leader who, regardless of the obstacles facing the organization, won't rest until the problem is solved.

It took me seven years to hit my stride as a communicator. During those seven years, I gave some boring speeches, and I felt discouraged at times. However, I was secure enough to keep taking the stage and honing my communication skills until I could connect with an audience. Had I been insecure, then the negative evaluations of others would have sealed my fate, and I never would have excelled in my career

4) Listening

Listen, learn, and ask questions from somebody successful who has gone on before you. Borrow from their experiences so that you can avoid their mistakes and emulate their triumphs. Solicit feedback, and take to heart what you're told. The criticism of friends may seem bitter in the short-term, but when heeded, can save you from falling victim to your blind spots.

5) Application

Knowledge has a limited shelf life. Unless used immediately or carefully preserved, it spoils and becomes worthless. Put the lessons you learn into practice so that your insights mature into understanding."

1. Which of these five insights do you relate with the most?

_____

_____

_____

_____

_____

2. Name a few qualities you feel a great leader should possess.

_____

_____

_____
_____
_____

3. Do you currently see yourself as a leader? Why or why not?

_____
_____
_____
_____
_____

Group discussion topics:

1) No one knows everything. If you're breathing, you can learn.
2) Knowledge is a tool. It doesn't help you at all if it's lying on the tool bench not being used.

PIC - Priorities, Integrity, Change

Read pages 19-21, 35 & 55-65 in *"Developing the Leader Within You"*

<u>Priorities</u>- *Developing The Leader Within YOU* page 19

It is not how hard you work; it is how smart you work. The good is the enemy of the best. From "The 80/20 Principle" (pages 20-21.)

Two things that are most difficult to get people to do are to think, and to do things in order of importance. Knowing these are common problems should have us looking at ourselves.

Prioritizing our projects can be difficult. Oftentimes, we can have so much going on at once that we don't know what to do first. Being overwhelmed, can lead to poor productivity, and the inability to focus. Here are a few tips to assist you with the job of prioritizing.

1. **LIST**: Gather everything that needs to be accomplished that day into one list, without thinking about the order or how you will do it all.
2. **URGENT**: Review your list, looking for anything that has an immediate deadline or must be completed today to avoid serious consequences. Note anything that is dependent on your portion being done to meet deadline.
3. **IMPORTANT**: Identify everything on the list that is important and of high value to your organization. It is helpful in determining importance to note how many people are affected by that item. Usually, the higher that number, the higher the importance.
4. **EFFORT**: Tasks that have seemingly equal priority can be ordered by effort involved to complete them. Experts say the one that will take the longest should be started first. However, go with your gut. Some people are motivated by ticking off several smaller ones first.
5. **CUT**: Any tasks that you won't get to that day, should be cut and moved to the list for the next day. This aids in staying focused on that day's work.

Priority Questions

1. Is thinking things through a challenge for you? What about prioritizing?

    _____
    _____
    _____
    _____
    _____

2. What are your top 3-5 goals this month? What steps will you take this during module toward these goals? Apply the tips above to your list to make it easier to accomplish.

    _____
    _____
    _____
    _____

ACTIVITY: Learning and utilizing the **S.M.A.R.T.** criteria will be most helpful in attaining personal and professional goals.

Read the article at this link:
http://topachievement.com/smart.html

3. What did you like most about this particular criteria? What ways could help you reach your goals?

    _____
    _____
    _____
    _____
    _____

Integrity – Developing the Leader Within YOU page 35

Integrity – (noun) the quality of being honest and having strong moral principles; moral uprightness. Doing what you say, walking the talk, staying above reproach

Integrity Questions

1. **Consistency**- Are you the same person no matter who you are with? **Y/ N**

2. **Choices**- Sometimes the integrous choice is the one that will be best for others, but not for you. Do you make decisions that are best for others when another choice would benefit you? **Y / N**
3. **Credit**- Are you quick to recognize others for their efforts and contributions to your success? **Y /N**

You may now be asking, "So what do I do to build it?" First, knowing a few factors that can cause a lack of integrity can be helpful. Fear plays a big role. The fear of not being accepted or liked or being vulnerable can cause a lack of integrity. Low self-esteem or lack of confidence can contribute, as can a need to feel in control. Sometimes we are simply modeling the environment we were raised within, and sometimes it comes down to poor communication skills. Whatever the reason, one can never have too much integrity. Consistently living an integrous life will build your self-worth, and opinion of yourself, which for many of us is very needed.

Here are some tips on improving your integrity.

A. Be willing to be vulnerable.
B. Surround yourself with people whose integrity and values you admire.
C. Make a list of your values and live them out.
D. Work on your self-worth and confidence.
E. Be intentional. Stand by your decisions and keep your agreements.
F. Be a student of yourself, staying aware of areas that need improvement.
G. Build your communication skills, maintaining honesty and kindness.

Change: Developing The Leader Within YOU pages 55-65

Knowing and accepting that we don't know it all is crucial to being a good leader. Being able to assess surroundings, and make changes is paramount, though.

Change = Growth
Growth = Good

Change can be a daunting thing or a very exciting thing. Part of your personal reaction to change does depend on your personality. But, there are other factors that govern your view of change, as well.

Past experiences, fear of the unknown, a deep desire for stability can be factors. Feeling as if the change is boing foisted upon you, can cause you to be resistant, as can failing to see the importance or necessity of the revision. The stress of the perceived upheaval this new improvement will cause, can definitely inspire you to think twice. Sometime people don't accept change because of tradition. The phrase, "That's the way we have always done it," drive me bonkers! That is no reason to maintain the status quo. Face it, if change didn't occur, we'd all still be crawling around, because we would have never taken the risk of learning how to walk.

In order to be a leader who embraces change, we need to know how we respond to change, and be willing to improve our response, if needed. A leader who is confident, and sure of the new innovation, will inspire confidence in his people. No matter how much good the new thing will bring, if the people aren't onboard, it is usually a waste of time.

Change Questions

4. How well do you embrace change? List the top few things that seem to get in your way.

_____
_____
_____
_____
_____

5. What can you do to help change your opinion of change?

_____
_____
_____
_____
_____

ACTIVITY: Write "attitude" with your writing hand on the left, and then with your non-writing hand on the right. The result written with your non-dominant hand is a picture of the kind of attitude we tend to have when we are doing something new.

HOMEWORK: Complete final project: Mission Statement.

YOU DID IT!

You were born for greatness!

Isaiah 43:18-19 - "Remember not the former things, nor consider the things of old. Behold, I am doing a new thing; now it springs forth, do you not perceive it? I will make a way in the wilderness and rivers in the desert."

YOUR VERY FINAL assignment, should you choose to accept the challenge, is create a mission statement for the next year of your life. It is not for the REST of your life, just simply the next year. Here's a few tips on mission statements:

A **MISSION STATEMENT** is the short-term goal: A single sentence that is tangible and has a specific goal. It should

- present a clear finish line that keeps people focused on a result
- verge on unreasonable
- connect with volunteers
- be grounded
- have an end goal that the ministry can achieve
- when the goal has been met, refocus and set the bar higher!

Here is a sample mission statement:

Helping Hands exists to provide healing and restoration to female victims of domestic minor sex trafficking (DMST) in a safe and loving family environment in order to redeem their identity and give them hope and a future.

Notice the first line states WHAT WE DO; the second line says WHO WE DO IT FOR; the third line HOW WE DO IT, and the last two lines WHY WE DO IT.

Below is a template to help you along this creative process. This can be answered according to a future goal you have, or geared toward your own personal calling. Write as many answers in the blanks as you can. Then create a sentence by combining all of your favorite options.

Who we are:

_____

What we do:

_____

Who we do it for:

_____

Why we do it (end goal):

_____

Write out your Mission Statement:

_____

_____

_____

_____

_____

Elevate Graduation

Student Name: _____

Mission/Vision Statement: _____

_____

_____

_____

_____

End Goal: _____

Personal Roadmap:

- 3 Month

- 6 Month

- 12 Month

Follow Up Dates:

3 Month	
6 Month	
12 Month	

Rebecca Bender 2014 ©

52029656R00070

Made in the USA
San Bernardino, CA
09 August 2017